SNAKES AND LADDERS

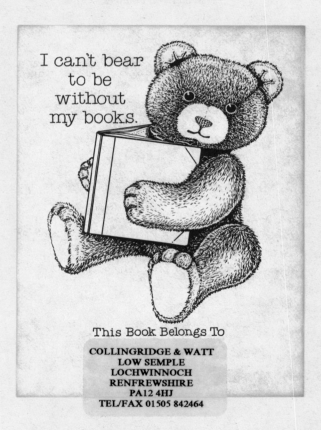

I can't bear
to be
without
my books.

This Book Belongs To

Gita Mehta

SNAKES AND LADDERS

Glimpses of Modern India

VINTAGE

Published by Vintage 1998

2 4 6 8 10 9 7 5 3 1

First published in Great Britain by
Secker & Warburg 1997

Vintage
Random House, 20 Vauxhall Bridge Road,
London SW1V 2SA

Random House Australia (Pty) Limited
20 Alfred Street, Milsons Point, Sydney,
New South Wales 2061, Australia

Random House New Zealand Limited
18 Poland Road, Glenfield,
Auckland 10, New Zealand

Random House South Africa (Pty) Limited
Endulini, 5a Jubilee Road, Parktown 2193,
South Africa

Random House UK Limited Reg. No. 954009

A CIP catalogue record for this book
is available from the British Library

ISBN 0 09 926822 1

Papers used by Random House UK Ltd are natural,
recyclable products made from wood grown in sustain-
able forests. The manufacturing processes conform to
the environmental regulations of the country of origin

Printed and bound in Great Britain by
Cox & Wyman, Reading, Berkshire

I should be sorely tempted, if I were
ten years younger, to make a journey to India –
not for the purpose of discovering something new
but in order to view in my way what has been discovered.

Johann Wolfgang von Goethe, 1787

Foreword

The traditional Indian game of Snakes and Ladders is
played by rolling dice to determine how many squares a
player can move his marker up a board, starting at square
one and finishing at square one hundred. Because of its
unpredictability it was one of our favourite games when
we were children. There was the element of chance determined by the throw of the dice. But more than that, the
actual board was suggestive of danger, an austere geometry
of squares broken by angled ladders and snakes with
yawning jaws. Landing at the foot of a ladder meant you
could climb it, sometimes moving thirty squares in a single
throw. That was the good part. You could also make it
all the way to square ninety-nine, only to encounter a
snake painted in lurid colours. Then you had to slide down
the serpent while your gleeful opponent streaked past.

Of course, like all ancient Indian games Snakes and
Ladders was devised for a purpose other than keeping
children amused on rainy afternoons and I have seen sixteenth-century cloth depictions of the game which once
hung in isolated Himalayan monasteries. Just as the Indian

board game of chess was designed to teach the strategies of war, so Snakes and Ladder was played ritually as Gyan-baji, the Game of Knowledge, a meditation on humanity's progress towards liberation.

India gained self-government in 1947. Living through our first half-century of nationhood has been a roller-coaster ride, the highs so sudden we have become light-headed with exhilaration, the lows too deep to even contemplate solution, as if the game of Snakes and Ladders had been invented to illustrate our attempts to move an ancient land towards modern enlightenment without jetti-soning from our past that which is valuable or unique.

Sometimes, in our glacial progress towards liberation from the injustices that make a mockery of political free-doms, it seems we Indians have vaulted over the painful stages experienced by other countries, lifted by ladders we had no right to expect. At other times we have been swallowed by the snakes of past nightmares, finding our-selves after half a century of independence back at square one.

Perhaps historians will make sense of India's early years of freedom. I find myself able only to see fragments of a country in which worlds and times are colliding with a velocity that defies comprehension. These essays are an attempt to explain something of modern India to myself. I hope others may also see in them facets of an extra-ordinary world spinning through an extraordinary time.

Dedicated to

'the sole country under the sun that is
endowed with imperishable interest for alien prince
and alien peasant, for lettered and ignorant,
wise and fool, rich and poor, bond and free,
the one land *all* men desire to see, and having
seen once, by even a glimpse, would not give that glimpse
for the shows of all the rest of the globe combined'.

Mark Twain, 1897

ONE

One

Freedom's Song

It was three o'clock in the morning and my mother was still dancing at the Roshanara Club in Delhi when her labour pains began. She was rushed to hospital and I was born an hour later.

Holding me in her arms, my godmother demanded that I be named Joan of Arc. She was a revolutionary, you see, like many of the other young people dancing that dawn. Styling themselves freedom fighters, frequently forced to go underground for their political activities against the British Empire, when they were not in jail they spent an inordinate amount of time dancing the rumba, the tango, the foxtrot, and hoping that the British departure from India was imminent.

My parents lived in New Delhi, the brand-new capital designed by Lutyens for a British Empire destined to last forever, but in barely twenty years the Empire was already looking rocky and my parents were providing sanctuary to so many Indian nationalists on the run from the police that an élite of freedom fighters across the subcontinent knew my parents' home as Absconders' Paradise.

On the morning I was born a consensus of opinion in Absconders' Paradise held that Joan of Arc lacked an Indian resonance. And so I was named Gita, or song. As in Song of Freedom, you understand, because it was the 1940s and it seemed that freedom was finally at hand. Their choice of name showed a premature optimism. Exactly three weeks later six armed constables arrived at Absconders' Paradise, manacled my father, and took him off to jail.

The handcuffs had to do with the pistols. A decade of Gandhian non-violence had not dislodged the British from India. These ardent young nationalists, mostly still in their twenties and impatient for freedom, had acquired arms from sympathetic nationalist officers in the Indian Army against the day when they might have to die on their feet rather than live on their knees. Indeed, a few years earlier my father's first cousin, a nineteen-year-old poet who had led the raid on the British Armoury at Chittagong, died on the steps of the Armoury in a volley of bullets rather than surrender, unaware that his wounded younger brother had already been captured.

As the handcuffs were placed on my father, he instructed my mother, under guise of taking farewell, to get rid of the arms. Otherwise it was a certainty that Father would find himself sharing a cell with his unfortunate cousin in the dreaded penal colony of Kala Pani – the Island of Black Water – one of the distant mass of Andaman Islands where only the most dangerous prisoners were incarcerated, and where conditions had been so unspeakable that half of the sixty-odd prisoners who shared my uncle's life sentence, when he was deported at the age of fourteen, ended up committing suicide in their cells.

Getting rid of the arms posed a problem for my mother.

Like many girls in Northern India she had been raised in purdah. Tutored in the seclusion of the women's quarters by a succession of women, including a Scottish governess, my mother's traditional education ensured that she could turn out a competent water-colour of the lakes of her native Kashmir, play the odd raga on the sitar, show familiarity with the allusions of classical Sanskrit, or recite Persian quatrains. But she lacked certain modern skills.

Early in their marriage, my father set about correcting this inadequacy. Displaying a nice sense of priority, and ignoring the considerable difference in their heights, he first taught my mother ballroom dancing. Then he taught her to play bridge. Then he put her on a bicycle, pushed it until she pedalled well enough to retain her balance, and deserted her. She cycled half-way around Delhi before she had the courage to dismount, but her one lesson made her a cyclist.

Father, who was by way of being an air ace, now decided that Mother should learn how to fly an airplane, and at the moment of his incarceration she was proving a demon at the controls of a Tiger Moth. *But the ability to drive* an automobile – so desperately required at that critical moment – was a skill which Mother lacked. As yet Father had only taught Mother how to reverse the two-seater Sunbeam Talbot convertible out of the long drive that connected Absconders' Paradise with the outside world.

Nonetheless, as soon as Father was frog-marched away, Mother chucked the pistols and rounds of ammunition into pillowcases, got into the Sunbeam Talbot and gamely reversed out of the gates as far down the road as she could go. Leaving the motor running she leapt out of the car, tossed the pillow cases into a ditch beyond a darkened pavement, reversed into a U-turn, and returned home, where, uncharacteristically, there were no revolutionaries to keep a eye on two small children bawling for attention, my one-year-old elder brother and myself.

The next day Mother discovered she had decanted the pistols outside the walled compound of the Chief Inspector of Police. Fortunately, even in that moment of high melodrama, my mother, with the miserliness of the good housewife, had been careful not to use her monogrammed linen, and the connection between the arms and Absconders' Paradise was never established.

As it happens, only a few months earlier Father had been handsomely complimented, even decorated, by the Vicereine of India for the large number of British civilians he had evacuated from Burma in the teeth of the Japanese advance during World War II. Landing in impossible terrain, making sortie after sortie accompanied only by an engineer, jettisoning fuel to accommodate even more women and children on the packed aircraft, Father had generally displayed that daredevilry which is later recognized as heroism but at the time is only the natural conduct of young men larking about with life and death.

Sentimentality is an early casualty of nationalist struggles. Father saw no paradox in keeping pistols for future use against the British even as he was risking his own life to save British lives. Equally, the British saw no paradox in jailing a man as a terrorist whom they had only recently lauded as a saviour.

The task of living with these ironies fell to my mother. For almost four years she followed my father from jail to jail, dragging two infants with her, smuggling letters into jail, sometimes in the soles of my brother's shoes – although my brother, with the self-importance of small children, sometimes insisted on showing the jailers his hiding place, thus lengthening Father's prison term.

After two years she deposited us in a convent in the hills so that she could better concentrate on trying to curtail Father's increasingly hair-raising attempts at escape, until that blessed moment when he broke his arm in several places and she prevailed upon a revolutionary doctor to personally set the arm. Upright. For months Father was frozen in the posture of a policeman stopping traffic because Mother feared her husband's height and his hell-raising temperament would make him an easy target for recapture and deportation.

Meanwhile Father was using his jail years to improve his cooking and his chess game, and to hatch schemes for destroying the British Empire. The plot dearest to his heart required him to become a textile magnate. Apparently textile factories used the same dies and chemicals that were required for the manufacture of currency. Father was convinced that within six months of his release he could flood the subcontinent in such a tidal wave of counterfeit currency that it would drown the British Raj.

Many years later, when India had been an independent country so long it was difficult even to imagine a British Empire, I telephoned my parents from Europe to say I was expecting a child. They were enthusiastic in their congratulations and demanded that I return to India for the birth. But of the long conversation I only remember the succinct observation, 'Then at least we will have lived to see our first grandchild born on Indian soil.'

That remark made me realize for the first time that my husband and myself had not been born citizens of a free India.

In an attempt to understand what it felt like on a

day-to-day basis to be a colonized people I asked my mother, 'What is your worst memory of living under British rule?'

'My worst memory?'

'Your absolute worst.'

My mother considered her answer for so long I thought she was sifting through memories too painful to express. My father's imprisonment; herself running from one official to another trying to gain his release; sending her children off when they were still babies to live in boarding-schools; deciding which of so many humiliating experiences had been the most humiliating.

Finally she said, 'When I was sixteen years old I remember walking down the railway platform with my father's oldest retainer to board a train to Lahore. Suddenly an Englishwoman sitting in a railway carriage put her hand through the window and pulled off the old man's turban. I was horrified that she could so casually insult such a dignified old man! I stood there thinking of the filthiest abuse I knew in English. Then I shouted up at her, "How dare you? You old hag!"'

'Did the police come for you?' I asked.

'Police? What are you talking about? This English-woman looked at me through the train window. She had red hair. And she said, "My dear, one day you will be an old hag too." That is my worst memory of the British Raj.'

Since traditional Indian mothers are not given to deadpan humour I could only take what my mother said at face value.

So I asked my father what his worst memory of the Raj had been. I expected him to tell me of his schooldays, when an irate police sergeant, for no particular reason except perhaps the heat, had smashed a truncheon on his head, splitting his scalp in a five-inch gash. Or similiar experiences, not so much for the pain inflicted as for the impotence of not being able to respond. Or at the very least, the months he had spent in solitary confinement.

Instead, Father said, 'Once I was asked to fly a British colonel and his adjutant to the North-West Frontier. As I was climbing into the cockpit he said, very loudly, "My God! I'm not going up in an airplane flown by a bloody native!" Of course, he didn't have any option. So I landed in a field about a hundred miles from Quetta, the hottest place in India during the summer. And it was damned hot in that field, without a tree for miles. The colonel was sweating and abusing natives, his face getting redder and redder in the sun while his adjutant nodded obediently.'

'What did you do?'

'Got back into the cockpit, told him to find someone who wasn't a bloody native to fly him, and took off, leaving him to walk to Quetta.'

Over the years I have found that no amount of wheedling can get my parents or their associates to talk about their suffering. They will speak passionately about the suffering of others. Indeed, a whole generation of the *jeunesse dorée* of Bengal, scions of some of India's most powerful and distinguished families, went into hiding in the docks of Calcutta, having joined the outlawed Communist Party during the Bengal Famine created by the commandeering of food supplies for the Allied forces in expectation of a Japanese attack on India. When the attack did not materialize, the food was released and found its way into the black market, where ordinary people could not afford to buy it. That winter of 1942 into the spring, while tons of food rotted away, nearly three million people starved to death, most of them on the streets of Calcutta.

Decades later, these doughty old nationalists are still enraged when they speak about such injustices. Decades later, they still take those injustices personally. But the injustices they themselves endured are simply brushed aside as part of the necessary price of becoming citizens of a free India rather than remaining subjects of a foreign Empire. And whenever they talk about those years of nationalist struggle they only joke and tell funny stories, as if it were bliss in that dawn to be alive but to be young was very heaven.

And perhaps it was. The nationalist movement broke so many of the shibboleths that constrained conventional Indian society. Women raised as my mother had been could never have hoped to live with such ease among so many extraordinary young men and women in an atmosphere of such excitement. It wasn't just the airplanes, the pistols, the deadly games of hide-and seek with the police, the unchaperoned socializing between men and women. Their desire for freedom propelled them out of the confines of their sheltered lives and society's notions of respectable behaviour into unknown worlds where they were forced to discover their own strengths.

For instance, my godmother was from a well-known Hindu family from Eastern India, but she had broken iron convention by marrying a prominent nationalist who was a Muslim from Northern India. Her mentor, modern India's greatest woman leader, Sarojini Naidu – who called Mahatma Gandhi 'Mickey Mouse' and who was herself described by Gandhi's biographer, Robert Payne, as 'exuberant, earthy, irreverent, improbable . . . one of those women who make the world glad' – had already shocked

Indian sensibilities by marrying beneath her own high caste.

Such women were fearless, whether they were on the barricades or bearding the King Emperor in his palace or leading marches against mounted police. Later, that same fearlessness would take them into the middle of the worst Hindu-Muslim riots in the most crowded Indian cities during the partition of the subcontinent into the two nations of India and Pakistan, where, unarmed and unaccompanied, they would attempt to stop the killings through sheer force of will.

It is a fearlessness I find hard to understand today. Their courage did not seem to be inspired by self-aggrandisement or ideological dogma or religious fervour – those certainties which usually fuel suicidal actions – and sometimes I wonder if they did indeed possess what Mahatma Gandhi called a kind of moral force.

Hoping to grasp the nature of their courage, I spoke to the uncle who had been sentenced to the penal colony of Kala Pani.

He was an affectionate man who liked to play the piano and in his seventies still displayed a childlike curiosity about the world.

But I was in absolute awe of him. Seventeen years incarcerated in a penal colony!

'Weren't you frightened when you heard your sentence?'

'Naturally. I was only fourteen years old. I had been shot in the ankle, tortured and interrogated for weeks before being sentenced to a lifetime of hard labour, put in chains and loaded onto the ship sailing to Kala Pani. Still, I don't think I really understood fear until we docked and I saw four British jailers in knee socks and starched white shorts cracking their whips on the sand, shouting, "This is where we tame the Bengal tigers!" '

Then he had smiled. 'I wouldn't recommend my life to everyone. But I think when you face fear every day for years, and are lucky enough to survive, you learn a little about its limits. In any case British rule was also a form of imprisonment. There was no freedom of speech, or of the press, or of congregation. At least now we are citizens of a free nation.'

I suppose on paper that is true. But in the fifty years that India has been a free nation the names of those who genuinely fought for freedom have been progressively excised from our history.

Instead, we have been bored to tears by overbearing leaders who have claimed that they are India, or, even worse, that India is them. And their sons. And their sons' sons, yea even unto nausea.

The latter claim, particularly, sticks in the craw, especially when they go to extreme lengths to make the claim stick, such as the wholesale imprisonment of anyone who begs to differ. And there has been too little fearlessness in defying them.

In fact, the most interesting evolution in independent India is the change from individual fearlessness in the face of social and political injustice to craven courting of those who possess social and political power.

It is a surprise when things are otherwise. I once called on a senior bureaucrat whose office was only three doors down from that of the then Indian Prime Minister, Indira Gandhi, who was already quite loopy, and who entertained a genuine conviction that her family owned India. Naturally, her intense obsession with an imagined inheritance had given rise to an equally intense paranoia about those who might deny it, and consequently her administration was coloured with many examples of tale-carrying, of ambitious courtiers reporting lies about their colleagues, and all the other spy-versus-spy paraphernalia of the would-be despot.

Wont to harangue the citizenry in public speeches with such lines as 'Remember! My father gave you freedom!' she did not take lightly to government officers with an independent turn of mind.

So I was astonished to hear this senior bureaucrat expressing his exasperation with the Prime Minister in such terms as 'dynastic' and 'paranoid' without a hint of self-consciousness.

'Should you be talking quite so loudly about the Prime Minister in this way?' I enquired with some admiration. 'After all, she does employ you.'

'She doesn't bloody employ me!' he snarled. 'The people of India employ me. Don't you ever forget it. This is my damned soil.'

Such bad humour is enough to make you want to cling to your Indian passport for another fifty years of freedom. At least that was the thought that crossed my mind when an immigration officer at New Delhi airport enquired how long I had been resident out of India.

At my reply, he stared in disbelief. 'And you are still carrying an Indian passport, madam? May I ask why?'

It was an occasion to be blunt. But I was in a land where ladies don't swear. So I couldn't bring myself to snarl, 'Because this is my damned soil. And don't you ever forget it!'

Two

Who's afraid of being Indian?

'Why does no one want to be an Indian?' the interviewer asks me, to the surprise of the other panellists sitting around the table.

We are broadcasting a radio show in London. It is early in the morning. I am staring in a bemused fashion at the person being interviewed before me. He has been introduced, I think, as a dentist from Birmingham. But he is dressed as an American cowboy. Ten-gallon hat, chaps, six-guns. Although it is a radio interview he has just demonstrated how fast he can draw his six-guns.

'Isn't it interesting that everyone wants to be a cowboy?' the interviewer asks the dentist as I find myself blinking into the barrels of two pistols. 'Tell me, why does no one ever want to be an Indian?'

The dentist is holstering his guns and misses the question, so the interviewer turns to me. 'Well, why do *you* think no one ever wants to be an Indian?'

'I suppose', I reply as I watch the dentist warily, 'some of us have it thrust upon us.'

There is a burst of nervous laughter from the other

panellists. They have registered the sari, the red spot on my forehead, the markings of another kind of Indian but no less capable of taking the innocent question as some sort of racial insult. But it would have interested the immigration officer who could not understand how, having had the opportunity to become a denizen of the First World, I had not seized the chance to do so.

Such incomprehension is not unique, as any immigration official from the First World will confirm. Among the most obvious trends in present history is the movement of people from colonial countries which only recently gained their freedom towards the very countries their forebears expended so much energy to expel. The question is why.

From my childhood I still have vivid memories of getting into slanging matches with other children about comparative nationalities. Our opponents were ruddy-complexioned, blond-haired children from the West wearing fancy blue jeans and crinoline skirts – it was the fifties – who jeered at us, a group of Plain Janes in well-oiled plaits and sober clothes that covered our arms and legs.

'What have you got but snakes and monkeys?' they yelled. 'Indians are just poor and dirty and backward!'

Goaded beyond endurance, we shouted back, 'Well, we built the Taj Mahal!'

'Hundreds of years ago!' they sneered. 'What can you do now?'

'Well,' we said. 'Well . . .'

Even then it was clear to us that we could be respected for the richness of our past, but were not given much chance of a future. After all, the grim figures of the present were the realities of our youth, a burden of social and

...ic disparities which even the most Herculean ...our seemed powerless to reverse. Whereas these ...onfident dwarfs from the First World only had to worry about what they were going to buy next. Damned unfair, we muttered. Why couldn't we be one of them?

In other words, why can't we all be cowboys? Why does anybody have to be Indian?

Because to be an Indian today is to be assaulted by the enormity of the tasks we have inherited with freedom.

There are too many of us.

Our literacy levels are too low.

Half of us live below the poverty line.

Corruption has become the standard among those who are in public service at every level. As Piloo Modi, a Member of Parliament, once pointed out to his offended colleagues, 'In India it is an indignity to post a letter, get a telephone, put a child into school, seek medical help, find a job, buy a train ticket.'

But I think it is astounding that India has a Parliament at all.

A sense of impotence differentiates us from the generation that fought for India's independence.

'What is the point of voting?' a man on the street replied when asked how he would vote during one of India's general elections. 'The Government is a flop, the country is a flop, and everything is just getting flopper and flopper.'

Yet we enjoy that supreme consolation of freedom – kicking the bums out. And seventy per cent of the Indian electorate avails itself of such consolation at every general election.

To me, one of the miracles of this war-weary century is India's continued existence as a democracy. A concept invented in Greece two thousand years ago for a tiny city-state has been expanded in India to include nine hundred million people in a gigantic debate on the future.

One out of every six people on the planet is an Indian – engaged in creating a mutually acceptable world. Reality, no matter how unpalatable, cannot be denied in such a massive public forum. With each election comes a greater demand for accountability, a greater insistence that problems be addressed. With each increase in accountability comes an increased sense of individual power, a refusal to settle for the injustices of the past. Such effrontery has already carried half our population, many who once lived below the poverty line, into the light of possibility. This has been achieved in the first fifty years of our freedom.

So when I am asked today, why bother to be an Indian, I cannot confess to any very noble reason. Just an avid curiosity about the future.

Can you imagine if, by democratic consensus, the other half of our population was lifted above the poverty line and we created a country in which every citizen is able to sit down at the table?

That's one-sixth of the human race.

Can you imagine what that would mean for India?

Can you imagine what that would mean for the world?

Three

My Damned Soil

The thing is, I am not sure what India is. Or, to paraphrase the *Rig Veda*, even *if* it is.

The closest I have ever come to a definition was when I was driving through a jungle in eastern India and chanced upon a wooden plaque nailed to a tree on which someone with an imperfect grip on the English language but an enviable self-confidence had painstakingly printed, WELCOME TO INDIA – LAND OF HOARY ANTIQUITE AND FABULOUS CONTRAST. And from the days of 'hoary antiquite' there is a story which suggests another definition.

The way this story goes, many centuries ago two of India's greatest sages met for a sort of spiritual showdown. One sage was a great ascetic who had achieved indestructibility after spending a lifetime performing the most arduous penances. Fittingly, he was known as 'The Diamond-Hard Ascetic'. The other was a poet who had done no penances at all, and yet was considered the holiest man in India. He was revered as 'The Field of Experience.'

Angered that the poet was respected more highly than

himself, the ascetic thrust a sword into the reluctant poet's hands, defying the poet to wound him. The poet obediently raised the sword and struck the ascetic a mighty blow. The sword shattered but made no mark on the ascetic. Then the Diamond-Hard One brought his own sword down on the poet with all his superhuman strength, hoping to cleave the Field of Experience in two. The sword passed harmlessly through the poet's body and the mortified ascetic acknowledged the poet as his master. Penances had gained the ascetic only strength. The Field of Experience had gone beyond strength.

It is a cliché to say that India is not really a nation. Certainly it is not a nation with the diamond-hard convictions of national identity which inspire many other countries. It is not even a single civilization. Rather, it is several civilizations in separate stages of development, coexisting despite their contradictions.

And yet, throughout my youth there was an annual agitation in the Indian capital when top-notch types would arrive in Delhi from all parts of the land to attend the National Integration Council, and discuss – unsuccessfully – what was required to forge India into a recognizable nation.

Those were the days of independent India's youth, when people in the West would aggressively demand answers from Indians to such depressing questions as 'When is India going to have a revolution?' or 'Why hasn't India had a Long March?'

Both the National Integrationalists and the Western interrogators failed to realize that to achieve these dramatic upheavals a country must have a cohesive identity – and India hasn't.

The annoying absence of an identity that can be controlled has always upset those in positions of power in India. It drove the bureaucrats of the British Raj crazy as they found themselves fighting a losing battle against what they saw as the chaos of India. It drove their imperial predecessors, the satraps of the Moghul Empire, into opium addiction. And the same frustrations are clearly evident in the present rulers of India, who struggle to centralize a land that has no centre but is only a Field of Experience.

Those who believe in the dialectics of materialism or the authority of history wander through the ruins of glorious empires and tell us India has learned nothing from her past. Others play statistical roulette and tell us India has no future. Professor John Kenneth Galbraith, sent by President Kennedy as American Ambassador to India, came up with a catchy, even accurate phrase when he described India as a 'functioning anarchy'.

For me, this lack of homogeneity which so threatens the assembly-line sensibilities of the end of the twentieth century is the essence of India's genius, her greatest strength. You may not be able to control what you can't grasp – but you can't destroy it either.

To take the obvious contradictions first. Most Indians view most other Indians as foreigners, and with considerable justification. The British only governed two-thirds of India. The other third was made up of over five hundred independent kingdoms, so the geography, the races, the languages, the customs of India have less in common with each other than do their equivalents among the actually separate nations of Europe or the Americas.

I once asked a man from South India who was working for an Indian diplomat in London if he felt homesick being so far from home.

'Not really,' the man replied. 'I am quite used to being abroad. Before I came to London I was working in Delhi.'

It was a reasonable answer. India is the sum of a million worlds enclosed by oceans on three sides, the mighty Himalayas on the north. Within these boundaries are voluptuous eastern cultures circled by paddy fields and western desert kingdoms locked in stone fortifications. Descendants of India's earliest inhabitants occupy the jungles sweeping through her heartland; three-thousand-year-old sacred cities still flourish on the banks of her immense rivers; merchant cultures still grow rich from her ancient ports.

So Delhi may be the capital of the Indian nation but the people of India see themselves as belonging to an Indian universe defying the vagaries of history. The physical features of their capital support the logic of this view. Delhi has been the centre of at least seven empires, each of whose emperors were addicts of monumental architecture, and even a casual drive through the city forces one to brood on the transience of *gloria mundi*.

Behind the huge elephant gates of a fortress known simply as the Old Fort because no one can quite remember who built it, archaeologists are excavating the ruins of what they believe to be the sacred empire of the Hindu religious epic, *The Mahabharata*. Down the road is the vast sandstone showpiece built to house the Viceroy of what was once the most powerful empire on earth, the British Empire. Further on is the mighty Red Fort that housed the Viceroy's predecessors, the Moghul emperors, who called themselves 'the Shadow of God on Earth' and gave audience from a Peacock Throne in gem-encrusted chambers – the same fortress from whose battlements the flag of an independent nation was first unfurled when a

India finally kept, in the words of India's first
nister, her 'tryst with destiny'.

estiny was political freedom, an assurance of
birthright. Only this defines the contemporary Indian.

Other definitions fall before the evidence. We are not of
a single racial origin. The Aryans of the northern plains
are distinct from the Dravidians of the south, and both
have little in common with the Mongol inhabitants of the
east. Not even language.

The Government of India officially recognizes seventeen
major Indian languages in which state business may be
conducted. Each of these languages possesses not just its
own ancient and contemporary literatures, not only its
own newspapers, radio and television programmes, its
own films, but an individual script. Then we have the
classical language of Sanskrit. On top of that we have over
four hundred other languages, some written, others oral.
And of course, as the joint language of administration, we
have English, a language which Indians have made
uniquely their own in more than two centuries of usage.

If speaking in tongues is a mark of divine inspiration
then surely India can claim to be the most divinely inspired
place on the planet. Yet linguistic politics is a sword held
to India's throat and every time some foolish chauvinist
demands the imposition of one of India's many languages
as the national language, the nation erupts in language
riots. Such passion in my view is just as it should be. To
impose a common national language, with its implications
of a common culture, on a country as richly diverse as
India would tragically diminish us.

And of all the elements which have contributed to our
diversity, nothing has so enriched the 'land of fabulous
contrast' as religion. Hindu, Christian, Muslim, Jain,

Parsi, Jew, Buddhist, Sikh – in India there is really no escape from religion. Every river, every lake, every mountain is the repository of some tale of divine mythology; every jungle is marked with flowers and a smear of vermilion showing where India's tribals have worshipped nature.

Hinduism is the religion practised by the majority of Indians, although 'majority' ceases to have a conventional meaning when one notes that over a hundred million Indians are Muslims, giving us the third largest Muslim population of any nation on earth. Our two-thousand-year-old Christian community claims that the first Christian missionary to reach India's shores was Christ's disciple Doubting Thomas, and that the Church in India began with him.

We have the tree under which the Buddha reached enlightenment, Hindu temples built under the guidance of the gods, mosques so vast that 70,000 faithful can kneel together on their prayer mats to say *namaaz*. The stupas and monasteries of the Buddhist faith are carved into our mountains. The stone colossi of the Jain religion dominate our hillsides. The Parsis have their Towers of Silence and Fire Temples which may only be entered by the followers of Zoroaster, the Sikhs their marble and gold Gurudwaras. There are the cathedrals of the Roman Catholics, the Orthodox churches of Armenians who fled the pogroms of the Ottoman Empire, the synagogues of the Jews. And there are the countless shrines which commemorate the countless holy men of India.

In Bombay there is a tree in the middle of a traffic island, gallantly defying the urban nightmare and admirably illustrating the poet W. H. Auden's definition of civilization as 'the degree to which diversity is attained, unity retained'. It is my favourite shrine, housing three separate faiths while the anarchy of Bombay's traffic hurtles oblivious around it. On one side of the tree is a white plaster Christian cross. On another is a small image of the elephant-headed Ganesh, the Hindu god of protection. On the third side is a small concrete altar on which worshippers place the Koran when they pray to Allah.

At our best in India, we still have a civilized tolerance that can accommodate three faiths in one tree-trunk because at its best the culture of India is like a massive sponge, absorbing everything while purists shake their heads in despair. Other cultures have sought to expel all foreign-devil influences from their shores. India has always shown an appetite for foreign devils, matched only by her capacity to make them go native.

It is as though we are unable to conceive of a culture strong enough to destroy us. Unlike China or Japan, the gates of India have never been closed, and perhaps this has given us a special stamina. Japan was the secret kingdom, the impenetrable civilization – but where have all the kimonos gone? In India we are still wearing our saris and our dhotis, not in defiant chauvinism but because quite simply that is how we dress, in spite of the fact that as late as the 1930s, when it was evident that the imperialist jig was up, an Indian official of the British Empire could still be fired if he turned up at his government office wearing native clothes.

So when I see painted on the walls of sixteenth-century Rajput villas pictures of the god Krishna playing his flute not to a herd of cows in a meadow but from the back seat of a Rolls-Royce, I feel reassured that Indian culture is still in business, that Krishna will continue to play his flute whether he is in a field, a Rolls or a rocket.

But as the rest of the world races headlong towards the bionic, sometimes I wonder if we will also be tempted by the siren songs of Disneyland and settle for a safe homogeneity. In fact, twenty-five years ago I stumbled upon what I then perceived as the end of Indian culture.

I was visiting the pillared edifice in Delhi that housed the state-controlled All-India Radio, the major patron of Indian culture after the court patronage of India's artists had ended.

Lost in a warren of recording studios I entered the wrong studio and found a young woman sitting behind a steel desk in a small sound-proofed cell. Her hair was covered with an embroidered veil. In the centre of her forehead was an enamelled ornament held in place by a line of pearls. Just visible under the silk folds covering her head were long ear-rings that swayed in and out of her hair as she sang. The manner of her dress and singing indicated that she was a *mushaira* girl, trained in the arts of singing and poetry from childhood, expected to hold cynical aesthetes in thrall by her ability to convert their remarks into poetic quatrains sung to melodic variations, without ever repeating herself.

The essence of her training would have been mastery of an audience, the catalyst to her artistry a dialogue with that audience. But the times had changed and here she was in all her finery, sitting on a wooden chair instead of leaning against cushions on a richly woven carpet, seducing a microphone dangling from the perforated sound-proofed tiles on the ceiling, her kohl-lined eyes frantically seeking a response from the recording engineer in his glass box, who was studying his dials, not her, as she plaintively sang,

The world speaks of permanence
But when I walked to the cremation ground
My path was crossed by a bridegroom.

Had she been performing her melancholy lament in front
of a live audience she would have been showered with
money and compliments. As it was, she just seemed camp.
An art that had to do with dialogue had been reduced to
the poutings of narcissism.

Even something as inconsequential as a *mushaira* girl
singing divertissements in an isolated and sound-proofed
room is antithetical to Indian culture because of our conviction that art is not just something displayed by the
talented to a passive audience, but rather that moment
when the artist, the audience, the subject, the discipline,
all combine to become something approaching religious
experience, a moment of mutual creation.

One of India's great sitar maestros has described how
he was trained to lead an audience to such perception
when he was learning to play the Bhairav, a morning raga
performed to herald the dawn. The Bhairav is a musical
meditation on the transition from darkness into light, cele-
brating the rebirth of the day as a rebirth of the spirit. But
in itself the raga is only a scale, so a musician's excellence
is assessed by what he can do with that scale through
improvisations that last more than an hour.

The sitar player's account of how he was taught as a
young boy to play this handful of notes is an illustration
of how the Indian artist learns his art. He and his fellow
students would rise at 3.30 in the morning. By 4.30 they
would be expected to be at their places in the courtyard
of the guru's house, where the guru would be waiting, a
bronze oil-lamp by his side. The pupils would sit before

him on white sheets spread on the flagstones, sitars balanced on their left shoulders, eager to prove themselves prodigies. The guru would ask the pupils one by one to play the first note of the raga. Believing this to be some sort of warming-up exercise the students happily complied. Then the guru would make them play the same note again. For three hours every morning the guru would allow his students to play that single note only, teaching them to contain the aspirations of an entire raga in a single sound.

Each month the guru allowed the students to add another note to their repertoire, until they understood that they were not learning music, but how to meditate. It was eight months before they were allowed to play the entire scale, two years before the guru permitted his most gifted pupil to perform the raga.

In his account of that first performance the sitar maestro records how those punishing hours of stilling his own mind, of being forced to listen to each note as if it were the primal sound, of having to concentrate on the transition from dark to light – through the different seasons – for two whole years, gave him an understanding beyond himself or his talents which he could reveal through music to the listener, a religious awareness he could share with his audience.

The same purpose moved those who carved the stone sculptures, built the great erotic temples, or cast the bronzes in India's cultural past. The measure of their excellence is the fact that centuries later their art is still venerated in worship, not isolated by mere admiration.

Today the Government no longer wields the total control it exercised for forty long years over Indian radio and television. So, in a sense, artistic freedom has increased. But in our changing world, new media require stars instead of artists, new audiences prefer sensation to meditation. The dialogue of live performance is giving way to the monologue of record, radio, television. Can Indian culture really withstand the twin challenges of electronic communications and marketing, when young Indians are dancing to hybrid music forms like Indi-pop and Bhangra-rock; when peasant farmers possess cellular telephones; when satellites are proliferating over our skies?

It is devoutly to be hoped that we rise to the challenge and continue to have a life outside the limited world of recording studios and museums. If not, we are in trouble. Preservation is not our game. As for decay, we are hardly conscious that it exists.

And yet there is a fecundity in Indian decay that suggests the possibility of coming attractions. We smell more of compost-heap than of the graveyard, showing an endless ingenuity in adapting progress to accommodate the human form.

An anthropologist once described to me a mass engagement ceremony he had attended in a desert area of Western India. Fifty girls from one nomadic tribe were being engaged to fifty boys from another tribe, the idea being that when the children reached maturity they would not have to race around the desert looking for suitable mates since they would now be assured of a future domestic life.

That night, in deference to the festivity of the occasion, the parents wore the traditional jewellery which the anthropolgist had come to record – globes of beaten silver fastened to the hair with thick, intricately carved silver chains. But their children wanted higher wattage. Impatient with their fathers' silver chains and globes, the sons wore light-bulbs on their heads, strings of electrical

Christmas decorations powered by batteries attached to their belts. The girls were thrilled. The desert glowed with lights of many colours. And the ethnic expert from the big city realized how patronizing his own attitude was. Until that night he had thought of these nomads not as people but as hangers for tribal artefacts.

In India we are still forced to remember that people are individuals as well as anthropological or economic statistics. The world has lived so long under the yoke of Malthusian projections that Indian humanity has become a dirty word, meaning only population explosions, though nothing has proved so damaging to modern India as the patronization of master-race economics with its real fear of the poor and therefore its unsaid but unmistakable view of the poor as subhumans who must be forced to accommodate the logic of economics.

The fact is that even if half of us dropped dead and the population ceased populating entirely we could not become some sanitized suburbia, never turn into Singapore. We are a continent not a city – a continent that has, despite its own inertia, the unwieldiness of its massive bureaucracy, the venality of its leaders, the centuries-old institutionalized injustices of its social systems, consistently proved the prophets of doom more wrong than right.

We were told we could never survive as a democracy, because a hungry man can have no understanding of freedom. I even heard the British humanitarian Malcolm Muggeridge say on a British television programme, 'People whose stomachs are empty have no idea what democracy means.' Fortunately a former British foreign minister was also on the programme and spoke for India when he succinctly observed that such views 'make me want to throw up'.

And if statistics have any magic, here are some to counter the prophecies of the pessimists. India is among the ten most industrialized nations on earth. We turn out five million university graduates a year. We have a space programme in advance of many western European countries. Most importantly, we are self-sufficient in food.

The reverse side to these statistics is that self-sufficiency in food has not been matched by efficiency in getting food to the mouths of the hungry. The huge increase in university graduates has not been equalled by the creation of jobs to absorb them. The ability to launch satellites into space does not disguise the lack of irrigation and electrification on the ground.

Even a casual visitor cannot fail to observe that the diversities of India's past are more than matched by the immense complexities of her present, her problems infinitely more complicated than the simplistic solutions offered either by her own leaders or by experts from abroad. Indeed, Mahatma Gandhi, whom many Indians call the father of the nation, once said that any solution to India's problems could at best be valid for about ten years.

Well, we've survived five times that number of years as an independent country and we still retain the privileges of freedom – a secret ballot, a free Press, an independent judiciary.

We haven't set fire to the past on the specious grounds that only the destruction of the past would allow us a future. We have not indulged in wholesale institutional savagery on the equally specious grounds that only cruelty to present generations will ensure Utopia for future ones.

And yet India progresses, a monumental juggernaut of contradictory realities.

Have we been lucky? Or, even, great? Who knows?
Indians don't. They only shrug and say,
'That is Bharat. That is India.'

TWO

TWO

Four

Banish Poverty

'You must have seen the people foraging through that huge garbage dump on the outskirts of Delhi,' the Indian paper tycoon remarked.

'The beggars, looking for food?' I asked. 'Of course I've seen them.'

But that was all I had done. Seen them, then quickly turned away, covering my nose although the car windows were up and the banks of the four-lane highway were planted with bougainvillaea bushes to hide a square mile of fetid garbage with vultures circling overhead.

'They're not beggars,' the tycoon corrected me. 'They are rag-pickers – supplying raw material to us in the paper industry.'

I was shocked. 'You mean people working in those subhuman conditions are on your payroll? You hire them to live like that?'

'Of course I don't bloody hire them,' he said in irritation. 'They collect rags and sell them to a contractor. If you are looking for a convenient phrase you might say these people are self-employed.'

Well, talk about the unacceptable origins of capitalism.

'Actually, it's only an extension of the kind of work they have always done,' the tycoon explained kindly. 'They're all untouchables by caste. Local sweepers.'

Intrigued by these self-employed people, so evidently masters of their own destiny, I got out of the car and made my way towards the tiny figures in the middle of that grey landscape.

The handkerchief covering my face did little to protect me from the fetid quicksand under my feet. Why hadn't I realized this garbage dump would not be solid ground? That I would be sinking into the effluvia from the deaths, marriages, examination papers, hospital refuse of a giant metropolis of nine million people?

Beyond the dump flowed the holy Jumna River. On the far bank I could see the stone battlements of the Red Fort, where languid Moghul emperors had once enjoyed the evening breeze in their marbled wind pavilions while their subjects promenaded on the river bank below. One emperor had even famously sighed, 'If there is a paradise on earth, it is this, it is this.'

Today, to the left of the battlements a power-station belched grey smoke into the air, colouring the mile of garbage a uniform grey like filthy flannel. Sunk to my knees in spongy refuse, not daring to look down to see what might be clinging to my legs, I ploughed my way towards a thin woman wearing a short peasant skirt and a torn jacket. She looked middle-aged but could as easily have been in her twenties. In one hand she carried a long iron spoke, hooked at the bottom, which she plunged into the waste. Further on, I could see other scavengers fishing up bits of rusty iron or stained rags. Children, their heads barely clearing the surface of the garbage, worked beside their parents.

The exhausted woman examined me suspiciously when I greeted her. Was I a government inspector who was going to challenge her right to be here? Or a do-gooder who would take away her children, contributing their pittance to the family's survival? The fact that I was only a voyeur seemed to reassure her and she leaned wearily on her spoke to talk.

Where was she from?

Rajputana. She used the old name for the Land of Kings.

Had she always done this kind of work?

Of course not. She had only come to the city after seven consecutive years of drought had forced her husband to sell their land to a money-lender. She was a Bhoomiya.

I looked at her in surprise. The Bhoomiya people were pathfinders. Traditionally they had guided travellers through the deserts and jungles of Rajputana – knowing every water source, every edible plant, every religious sanctuary. They were paid in arable land, which their families cultivated while they delivered wayfarers safely to the next stop on their journey – until trains, buses, telephones had made the work of guides irrelevant.

The other rag-pickers were circling us warily. My presence had made them curious. Now they joined our conversation. A small boy was pushed forward by his mother.

He is a Bhat, the scavengers told me, the community of bards who once held mythic power over kings. Only Bhats had the right to recite the genealogies of royalty, or to convert great feats of battle and honour into the epic poems that were then recited throughout the countryside.

'Once our recitations began a royal coronation,' the

woman said, gently cuffing the child on the side of the head. 'Now look at my child's fate. We teach him the historical poems, otherwise they will be forgotten. And he shouts them aloud to frighten the vultures away while he looks for rags.'

I thought of the tycoon's casual observation that these people were local sweepers who had chosen to become scavengers, but sinking in the quicksands of the Indian capital's refuse, I was hearing tales of displacement from all over India.

Here was a woman from a riverside fishing village in Eastern India. During a heavy monsoon rains the swollen river had burst its banks and submerged her village. By breaking stones for roads, she and her husband had worked their way across India until they reached the capital – a thousand miles away from the lush delta of their native land.

Two girls told me they were tribals from central India. The dense jungles which had once supported their community had been destroyed first by lumber merchants, then by stone quarrying, and they had been sold by their parents to a man looking for cheap labour to work in the city's construction sites. When the building was complete he had left them to survive on their own and they didn't know where to find their parents, now working in some unknown part of India as bonded labour.

Next to them a girl from South India shyly explained that her father had been a craftsman. But three bad monsoons in a row meant the villagers could no longer afford to buy his wooden carvings. To feed his family, her father had been reduced to selling his tools, one by one, until he had none left. The family had begged for work from one village to another. They had stopped here, and her father worked as a stone mason now.

'Can't you see there are no men here?' the women asked. 'While we sift through other people's filth our men are all breaking stones for the new highway. That's what the last five years have done to us.'

'What happened five years ago?'

'Haven't you heard of the Remove Poverty programme?'

Of course I had, like every other Indian during Mrs Indira Gandhi's time as Prime Minister.

Throughout the seventies the message REMOVE POVERTY had been blazoned across the country on huge banners, on billboards and posters and graffiti smeared across walls. How could anyone have ignored it? But how had that brought them here?

'The politicians said they would remove poverty and give us jobs, so we voted for them. But when we got here they didn't want to meet us. We managed to feed ourselves by working on building sites. Carrying bricks. Mixing concrete. We lived in huts made from things that other people had thrown away. Then the country's bosses decided Delhi must look beautiful. From Remove Poverty their slogans changed to Remove the Poor.'

They laughed, pointing at each other. 'The poor are not beautiful, as you can see. While we were at work the bulldozers flattened our huts with all our possessions inside them. We were put in buses and taken thirty miles out of town where there is no work. No water. No food. Nothing to protect our children from the weather. Now we have fallen to this. But we fill our stomachs somehow. Thanks to him.'

'Who?'

They pointed across the four-lane highway. 'The Contractor.'

Behind a high bank of purple bougainvillea bushes was a shanty – two pieces of canvas stretched on poles to provide a little shade for a bed made from a discarded wooden door and covered with a threadbare cotton quilt. I made my way past piles of garbage and the tall bulrushes that lent them an almost elegant air. The pastoral element was increased by the mewling of puppies nestled for warmth in a bundle of rags. As I came closer the refuse took on a visible identity – plastic and polythene in one heap, rags in another, broken glass in a third. A fourth contained twisted shapes of rusting and bent iron.

A transistor radio was blaring popular film music over the traffic noise as the Contractor invited me in. He was an alert-looking runaway from a bonded labour camp in Bihar on whom fortune had smiled. A quarter of a million other bonded labourers working without wages to clear their debts were not so lucky.

But the Contractor had somehow managed to flee the money-lender demanding repayment of a loan taken by his grandfather, which his father and himself had repaid many times over in rapacious interest rates that placed the original debt beyond hope of clearance.

He even had his own house now – number 357 in a resettlement colony. It was actually only a mud hut but he called it his 'flat' and with equal pride he referred to this shanty as his 'office'.

'I know I deal in filth,' he said ruefully. 'But filth is my Laxmi. My Goddess of Wealth. If I don't stay here the rag-pickers can't bring me their goods. They already spend one third of their daily earnings just to take the bus to get here. That's what the Government's great Remove Poverty programme achieved. I give the poor wretches credit. But I have too many debtors. Many of them will never be able to repay me. Then I will be forced into picking rags again.'

In spite of the fact that he was now a money-lender, the spectre of returning to the garbage dumps haunted the Contractor. His office was an illegal construction. Government bulldozers could appear on the horizon at any moment.

Beyond the discards from an urban world stretched fields of young wheat, the green of manicured lawns. I could see veiled women in brightly coloured long skirts with brass pots balanced on their heads walking towards a well. Picturesque peasants in turbans tended their oxen or piled hay into high wooden carts. This serene rural landscape was the sleight of hand by which India could make even poverty acceptable. But the truth was, a few bad breaks and the picturesque peasants could join the faceless transients across the highway trying to make a living from the steaming grey garbage dump.

And how many stories of wasted human lives were there in this place? I asked a medical officer who worked among the slum dwellers.

At first he tried to give me the Government line. The rag-pickers were making a valuable contribution to the recycling industry. When I pressed him he finally admitted, 'We have no means of counting the number of people who are working as rag-pickers even in Delhi, let alone the rest of the country. Are there hundreds of them? Thousands? No one really knows. Actually, no one has tried to find out. They are a floating and faceless group of people. But at least give them this. They do something. They do not beg.'

A sanitation official in the Delhi Municipal Corporation

honest. 'We great Indians! It has become second
us to tolerate what is beneath human dignity in
ust so long as we ourselves remain untouched by
it. These people would not be collecting and selling dirt if
the Government could create other jobs for them. But the
Government is happy spending fortunes to make sure that
only slogans are heard by every Indian.'

Then he added bitterly, 'Imagine if all that money was
spent on giving them decent work.'

Five

Banish Charity

'When do you next get paid?' a friend asked me one evening, adding severely, 'Make sure you give the money to me.'

I stared pointedly at her jewellery. 'And why should I do that?'

'We are trying to buy some women out of bonded labour.'

I wasn't as surprised as I might have been by her bluntness. I knew she had worked with women in the industrial city of Ahmedabad who earned their living in circumstances no better than the garbage dumps of the nation's capital a thousand miles away.

Except for one thing. These women owned their own bank.

In the early fifties, years before feminism became a catchword in the West, the poorest women in Ahmedabad had pooled the meagre sums they earned by scavenging in refuse dumps, pulling hand-carts, selling rags, breaking stones for roads, carrying bricks in cane baskets on their heads, and started their own co-operative bank. They called themselves S.E.W.A., the Self-Employed Women's Association.

Their bank enabled them to take out loans and invest in such things as a sewing machine to make garments to sell. As soon as one group's initial investment was returned, another group of women took out another loan to start another cottage industry and become economically secure. Some members borrowed money to join training facilities and gain skills which would later allow them to form their own small commercial units. Others continued to ply their usual trades. But they were no longer hostage to money-lenders eager to turn their despair into limitless profit. Their own bank stood between them and such exploitation.

It was no accident that S.E.W.A. should have started in Ahmedabad, the capital of India's western state of Gujarat, where the trading energy of Britian's East India Company combined with the commercial skill of Ahmedabad's prudent merchants to make the city a centre not just of the textile trade but also of union activity. By the turn of the century, workers in its many textile mills had formed the Textile Labour Association, one of India's oldest and best organized labour unions, blessed by Mahatma Gandhi, whose ashram was on the outskirts of the city. Perhaps Gandhi's proximity moved the daughter of a rich man to unionize the workers in her father's textile factories, where conditions were so terrible that workers were happy to spend their entire week's wages getting drunk on country liquor sold from stills conveniently set up outside the factory gates on pay-day. When they got home they soundly beat their wives for asking for money to buy food for the children.

But the wives couldn't feed their children by working

in the city's many factories. Women employed i
organized sectors of Indian industry were rare. Even t
fewer than four per cent of unionized labour are women,
their numbers shrinking every year as men force them
from protected work-places in the intense competition for
limited jobs that are the dream of millions of 'casual
labourers' scratching a living on the very edge of survival.
Most women, and also their children, belong to the huge
population of unorganized labour, made homeless by
drought and debt, vulnerable to any exploitation in its
migration from the countryside to the city in search of
work.

This vast shifting sea of poverty has become the focus
of increasing numbers of voluntary organizations, often
led by women. In Ahmedabad the desperate wives, only
one step away from prostitution in the struggle to feed
their families, were urged by a young middle-class woman,
Elaben Bhatt, to form a union. The Self-Employed
Women's Association was founded in 1952. Today
S.E.W.A.'s bank in Ahmedabad boasts twenty-five thousand savings accounts, owned by its thirty thousand
members.

The acronym S.E.W.A. means service in Hindi, and
branches can now be found all over India. In the north it
has enabled sequestered women from the most orthodox
Muslim families to set up embroidering units and earn
enough to educate their children and still keep money
aside for the day they might be peremptorily divorced with
a verbal dismissal of 'Talak' by their husbands. In the
south it has helped low-caste Hindu women to break
the chains of illiteracy and start small businesses, marketing their crafts. From the hill communities of the east
to the desert communities of the west, units of S.E.W.A.

have encouraged self-employment and economic independence among women. Its members have created their own crèches and schools and medical dispensaries, taught each other hygiene and midwifery and nursing. Now the association is held up to the world as an example of self-help, to be imitated by poor nations everywhere. And it has led to numerous imitations in India itself.

One such imitation was formed in Delhi by six women working in different areas of craft development, enraged that the unique skills and art forms which are the glory of India's handicrafts had been reduced over the years to unusable bric-à-brac sold on city pavements by ignorant middlemen eager to exploit the tourist and 'ethnic' markets. Though themselves from privileged backgrounds, the women called their organization Dastkar, one who works with his hands, and their goal was the continued employment of craftsmen who were losing their livelihoods to factory-made products.

Dastkar was aware that craft is still India's second largest employer after agriculture, with a whole government department to look after its interests, the Handlooms and Handicrafts Board of India. After all, before mechanization, all goods had been manufactured by hand and India's thousands of differing worlds even now produce a huge span of distinctive handicrafts, often using highly sophisticated processes and affording vast numbers of women a livelihood. But today, the laboriously handmade products must compete with mass production and sophisticated marketing techniques to attract not just city dwellers but also villagers dazzled by the advertisements they see every day on their television screens.

Convinced that no amount of government protection could make people buy what they didn't want, Dastkar asked itself how it could help craftsmen to survive in the new market-place. Commercial and marketing expertise were the obvious answers. And it was not something village artisans possessed.

By working intensively with groups of artisans to produce crafts accommodated to modern usage; by teaching them accounting, book-keeping and how to acquire competitively priced raw materials; by taking artisans who have never ventured outside their villages into the cities to see for themselves what the consumer wants to buy, Dastkar is trying to develop modern markets that can be sustained.

One of the original founders was the friend who was now demanding my money.

'Who are these women you are trying to help, anyway?' I asked, putting up a fight to keep the money I needed for a trip to the south.

'Tribal women and their kids. They are working as bonded labour in a silk-weaving centre, practically chained to their looms.'

My trip to the south evaporated in fumes of momentary guilt.

'It's not very much,' I apologized, as I began signing travellers' cheques.

She palmed my money, observing acidly, 'Dollars go a long way in India.'

A few weeks later I returned to Europe, and heard nothing further from her.

It was eighteen months before I saw my friend again, at a rather grand dinner party in the Indian capital.

Dodging ambassadors and businessmen busily discussing the opening up of the Indian economy and whether the unleashing of market forces could make India into another Asian tiger, I caught up with her at the buffet table.

'Oh, I've been meaning to write to you,' she said in an off-handed way. 'But I've been busy.'

I was rather hurt. I felt she could at least have acknowledged my gift as being helpful. I didn't know that her organization was into self-reliance, not gratitude. Or that they ran forty units all over the country with a total capital base of only fifteen thousand dollars.

Noticing my dismay she relented. 'The money bought about one hundred and sixty women and their families out of bondage.'

I was stunned. I had only given her a few hundred dollars. 'One hundred and sixty women?'

'How big do you think the original debts were, for goodness' sake?' she asked, irritated. 'Two hundred or three hundred rupees, that's all.'

Now I knew the price of human life in India. Indeed, one stark analysis of bonded labour by the Indian School of Social Sciences showed just how much you could get for your money. In a single northern village Farmer Minu had borrowed Rs. 500 ($14) to buy food and was still working off the interest on his debt after seventeen years. Farmer Nanda had borrowed Rs. 100 ($3) for food and had already laboured without wages for twelve years. Farmer Sukha had worked ten years for a loan of Rs. 20 (75 cents) to buy a wooden box.

'What are the women doing now?' I asked my friend as she examined the dishes on the buffet table.

'They were determined to compete with their previous owners so we loaned them money to buy their own looms and weave their own silk.'

To imagine such courage you have to imagine the cruelty of their owners, men capable of buying other human beings and feeding them just enough so that they and their children can keep on working, while their husbands are used as beasts of burden elsewhere.

She speared a leg of chicken and put it onto her plate. 'In fact I've just come back from Bombay, where we have had an exhibition of their work.'

'Did you manage to sell it?' I asked with proprietorial concern.

'Oh, it wasn't for sale, just display for future orders. They haven't got anything left to sell. Everything the women produce is of such high quality the exporters grab it.'

She chewed at the chicken leg, oblivious to the impact her story was having. 'In fact, the men who used them as slave labour are now offering to buy their output at twice the price the exporters pay because the quality is so good.'

'Are they making money?'

She nodded, her mouth full.

'Well, what do they do with their money?' I persisted.

She wiped her lips. 'Send their kids to private schools. They think that if you pay for education instead of going to a government school your kids will get a better education.'

'Can I give them some more money?'

She was annoyed. 'Certainly not. They don't accept charity. Six months ago they paid back every penny of your money. Now they are giving us money to loan to other women. Nearly as much as you did.'

Two gentlemen, complaining about India's economy, forced their way between us to reach the table.

'We are caught in a vicious cycle of poverty,' one stated as he reached for a plate.

'Our tax base will never be large enough to support our population,' the other agreed. 'There's nothing we can do about it.'

My friend had already turned away or she could have told them they were wrong. After all, she had just finished telling me how one hundred and sixty enslaved women had gone from bondage to philanthropy – or was it banking? – in a single year. And unlike us, they didn't even know the meaning of the words.

Six

Re-inventing the Wheel

The spinning-wheel, long the centre of the Indian flag acknowledges that textiles are a living Indian art form still producing masterpieces equal to the past. But it also highlights the great debate in India about the traditional worker's function in our future.

Two tales from Indian mythology illustrate what the weaver means to India. The first story is about the Mother Goddess of the subcontinent, who one day took the form of a cosmic spider and began spinning a web of cotton thread. The web grew until it covered India, and still the goddess spun. Finally her immense web reached beyond the boundaries of the Himalayan mountains to enmesh the god of the Aryans – a god of progress and mechanical skills – binding him to India.

The myth of India's spider goddess and the Aryan god of machines is an uncanny foretelling of the European connection with India. Europe may have come East looking for spices but within decades Europe was inextricably bound in the web of Indian textiles. Bandana, chintz, muslin, calico, all were Indian words and techniques. From the rich hangings woven with threads of gold and silver which adorned the homes of European aristocrats to the bandanas worn by the slaves working the cotton and sugar plantations of the Americas, from the fine muslins which provided the Barbary sashes of the gentlemen of North Africa and the turbans of the nobles of the Turkish Levant to the chintz furnishings favoured by English ladies who dressed in calico lawn, it was the magic worked by the hands of the Indian weaver which created fortunes of such enormity that the nations of Europe fought for supremacy over India's cloth.

When Britain won the last battle for supremacy, the wealth flowing from the trade in Indian textiles turned a British trading company into the greatest empire on earth – which in its turn imported those gods of progress, the machines of the Industrial Revolution, into India.

The second myth is from the Indian epic, *The Mahabharata*. A beautiful and virtuous queen is lost by her husband in a gambling game to an evil king. The captive queen is brought into the king's audience chamber, where he is sitting upon his throne surrounded by nobles and soldiers. The king demands that his prisoner be stripped naked before the lustful eyes of the assembly. The laughing guards grab the queen's garments and begin to pull. Weeping for her modesty, the queen begs the gods to protect her honour and lo, even as the guards pull at her clothes, the fabric multiplies. The guards continue pulling but there is no end to the queen's garments. Billowing cloth covers the pillars and arches of the audience chamber until it reaches the dome above the king's head.

Prisoner queens may belong to ancient mythologies but it was in the harsh political realities of this century that

Indian nationalists again used cloth to defend India's honour, calling it 'the livery of our freedom'.

Raw cotton exported from India to the mills of Manchester and Lancaster was robbing Indian weavers of the source of their income, so homespun cloth woven in defiance of the power looms of the British Empire became the uniform of the Indian nationalist. Later it would become a symbol of self-reliance for free India.

Ironically, the earliest factories Indians were permitted to own by their British masters were textile mills. In the decades that followed, capital and technology generated from those early textile mills led to such wide-scale industrial expansion that India is today numbered among the ten most industrialized nations on earth.

This precise paradox – craft or machine, an ancient culture or contemporary progress – haunts India today. A large school of Indian thought believes the spinning-wheel as the centre of the Indian flag is symptomatic of all that is backward in India. Symbols once useful in expelling a foreign empire and its exploitations are now dangerous anachronisms in a country where – so the argument goes – wealth must come from increasing and more efficient mechanization.

But eighteen million Indians feed themselves from the profits of their handlooms, a further five million Indians earn their livelihood as craftsmen of a specifically Indian culture. How are they to co-exist with the pressures of modern economics and life-styles? And if this avenue of employment is closed can India ever hope to create factory jobs for twenty-three million additional workers?

Perhaps the answer to such questions can still be found in mythology, because there is a happy ending to the myth about the spider goddess of the Indian subcontinent.

Having trapped the foreign god of mechanization in her web, the goddess becomes mother, wife and daughter to progress.

Like the spinning goddess, Indian weavers have been the mother to Indian industry, the wife to Indian nationalism. The odds are that they will succeed in becoming heirs to modern India's progress. They have done so in the past. The scientific developments which dealt the death blow to so much Indian culture have constantly reinforced India's textiles. The dyes used in the woven fragments which survive from India's earliest archaeological remains, the Indus Valley Civilization, are still the colour spectrum which defines India: ochre, red, black and the legendary indigo. Experiments in extracting colour from plants led to the creation of these first dyes. Five thousand years later, experiments in recreating this colour palette chemically led to the growth of India's pharmaceutical industries.

As for mechanization, already India's weavers have absorbed some of the processes of the machine. But machines cannot duplicate an evolving world, and Indian weaving keeps abreast of Indian civilization only because the genius of India's weavers has proved great enough to contain that span.

The same knowledge that created the rich brocades worn by the emperors of China and Byzantium creates the brocades worn by Indian brides and grooms today. The same skills which produced the 'woven winds' worn by the Roman emperors – those prized muslins which wrapped the body of the Buddha when he attained Nirvana, referred to by the Moghul emperors by such names as 'morning dew' and 'cloth of running water' – are the skills which produce the muslins modern Indians wear in the punishing heat of summer. The same expertise that could weave wealth into beauty causes Indian brides today to preserve trousseaus woven with gold thread, so that in time of necessity they can burn the fabric and sell the gold.

Painted fabrics which must not contain a single flaw in the weave are still hung seasonally in Indian temples, acts of devotion by master weavers. The Muslim weaver-embroiderers of Northern India who weave the ninety-nine names of Allah into their work still see no contradiction in weaving brocade vestments worn by the Pope, regarding each textile as a form of prayer.

Waves of migrant weavers, displaced by industrialization, weave their homesickness into their fabrics, and those who buy them buy woven epics of dislocation. Tribal weavers use the brush and the loom to record the history of their travels, their work treasured by the anthropologist.

The knowledge of colours and cultures as they change with India's geography and peoples – the yellows of northern springs and wheat and mustard harvests, the whites and ivories of southern summers, the green of eastern rice fields and the seasons of desire, the old rose-pinks and musk-blues of Islam, the shades of indigo that denote the fury of the monsoon and the playful god of Brindaban, the differing shades of red that tell the varying constancies of lovers, the silvers and enamelled golds of royalty – these are the raw material of India's weavers. The designs and images that reinforce the meaning of colours and textures – these are the cultural province of India's weavers.

The paradox is this. Global mass production may seem an answer to poverty, but only a living culture can generate sustained wealth. There is a further para twenty-three million craftsmen depend on India's culture for their living, India's very culture depends on giving them a living.

Without our craftsmen we would be indistinguishable from any other country, our unique multiplicities limited by the machine. In the end machines can only reproduce a culture, they can't invent one – and who is going to produce machines fast enough to reproduce the fabrics created by the encyclopaedic knowledge, the endlessly changing adaptations of eighteen million weavers?

Seven

Food For Thought

I once saw a famine in the making. For three years the monsoon rains, life and death to rural India, had failed and there was drought in the state of Maharashtra. Crops had withered, livestock had starved, village wells were dry. By 1973, the third year of the drought, children were dying of hunger.

In the towns there was no power or running water. The reservoirs had sunk so low that in Aurangabad, a city of two million people, there was only enough drinking water for two days. When I arrived, I found its residents preparing to join the exodus which had already clogged the roads leading to the state capital, Bombay – where one out of every seven people was living on the streets.

To halt the exodus, the Government was tackling the situation on a military footing. Food donated from the overflowing granaries of the United States was being airlifted to remote villages. Mile-long lines of bullock carts bearing kerosene drums filled with drinking water were trundling down the roads in the opposite direction to the refugees. A textile mill owner had opened kitchens across the state serving a diet of his own devising that contained enough protein and calories to sustain a human being for at least twenty-four hours. Famished villagers queued at his kitchens while government radio railed against their obstinacy in refusing American grain, to which their palates were unaccustomed.

One of India's most distinguished political cartoonists and myself accompanied a district commissioner to a village in the epicentre of the drought.

Sitting on the caked ground outside their huts, emaciated village women were sifting through the wheat piled in heaps by their sides. They shook their cane trays furiously in a kind of hypnotic rhythm like the sound of *mariachis*, oblivious to the wailing of their children. Every few seconds they would stop, pick a grain out of the tray and put it to one side.

A bullock cart rolled to a stop on the outskirts of the village. The children stopped crying to crowd around the cart, holding out clay cups for water, cupping their hands to catch drops splashing from the cart onto the brown dust blowing across the ground. The women shouted at the children to fill the earthenware pots stacked outside the huts so that their fathers would have water to drink.

'Where are your husbands?' I asked the women, seeing no men in the village.

'Digging an irrigation canal.'

'In a drought?'

'For the next rains, if they ever come. Food for Work, the government officers call it. When our men build roads or dig canals they are paid in food.'

They shook their basket trays angrily. 'Poisoned food.'

The political cartoonist was sketching the white-turbanned farmer pulling at the bullock's horns to direct the animal back onto the road. The children deserted the cart to peer over his shoulder at the images forming on his white paper.

'Take my photograph,' they shouted, pushing each other out of the way to get closer to the artist, pleased to show off their knowledge of technology.

'Take my photograph too!'

'And mine!'

As he patiently drew quick sketches for the children I watched the women monotonously sifting their grain, picking out seeds from the wheat and placing them carefully in containers.

I couldn't understand why the women were engaging in such fastidious preparation when their children were hungry. 'Why don't you just cook it?'

'We don't want to die,' they answered wearily.

'Look!' A woman held up a handful of the separated seeds so that I could see for myself. 'Datura in the wheat.'

Safe for animal consumption, poisonous to human beings – the grain donated by the United States was cattle-feed.

Still, when you are starving you take what you can get.

I, on the other hand, was being given more than I could possibly consume. Enough to keep ten families fed at every meal. Enough liquor to keep ten men intoxicated for a week. A private airplane to fly me around the state. Cars to drive me to the worst sites of the drought. I was working for a British television company, you see. The cartoonist shared my privileges. He was working for a British newspaper. Because of our foreign employers we were honorary foreigners, travelling with the foreign journalists. So we shared in all the luxuries by which we in the Third World seduce the First World into paying attention to our problems.

This business of trying to impress the First World has cost the Third World dearly.

In the thirties a European journalist once asked Mahatma Gandhi, 'How can I understand India?'

'Study her villages,' Gandhi replied. It was an obvious answer. After all, three quarters of India lived in villages.

But the West had become wealthy through industry, and in the fifties Prime Minister Nehru and his advisers came up with a bold new plan to take India's bullock-cart economy into the machine age of the twentieth century. If Five-Year Plans and state-controlled industry were the magic bullets of development used by China and Russia, we would also channel our resources into massive industries owned by the state to create jobs. If America was building gigantic hydro-electric projects like the Boulder and Cooley dams, we would also build huge dams to provide power for our dream of mechanization. If every year we were importing food to stave off famine, then that was the price a poor country had to pay for progress. After all, we had always had famines.

It took a new Prime Minister, Shastri, to notice that our obsession with state industry was too expensive. More than factories, Indians needed to eat. Perhaps the fortunes we were borrowing to import food might be better spent helping Indian farmers to grow food. After all, in the vast sweep of the Indo-Gangetic basin we had the most extensively cultivated alluvial plain in the world. Further south we had the fertile volcanic soil of the great Deccan plateau. Actually, we had as much cultivable land as China without China's population, and a population density even today only slightly higher than Germany's, much lower than Japan's, leading the American Overseas Development Council to acknowledge 'India has a natural endowment for food production very close to that of the United States.'

Prime Minister Shastri chose a propitious moment to turn India's focus back to agriculture. It was the sixties and world scientists had achieved a breakthrough in crop production – high-yielding hybrid seeds for wheat and rice, the two staple foods of Indians.

Everyone said that it would take years of coaxing to make the cautious, backward, suspicious Indian farmer use them. Instead, our newspapers were soon printing stories of burly Sikh farmers breaking into Punjab research laboratories in the dead of night to steal the miracle wheat seeds and plant them before the next rains. In the south scientists were complaining they had no more seeds with which to experiment on Indian soil because their rice samples had mysteriously vanished.

It was the beginning of the Green Revolution.

In the years that followed the monsoons were still unpredictable, the rains still failed and we still had droughts. But within a decade we were able to feed ourselves. Another decade and we were exporting cereals. Ten years after that we were exporting a quarter of our agricultural produce. The Green Revolution had changed India forever.

Yet millions of Indians were still hungry, millions of dispossessed villagers were still migrating to the cities. We were spending fortunes on rural development but more than half our water, our most precious resource, was being lost every year to floods and evaporation caused by deforestation and mining and quarrying, while half our villages still had no drinking water.

A huge burst of effort was needed to consolidate our gains. Better irrigation, soil conservation, primary education, health facilities – these could change the face of rural India.

These – and effective land reforms. After all, we were a young nation of ancient inequalities where absentee landlords had owned vast hereditary holdings farmed by tenant farmers, who paid a third of their produce to the landlord and another third to middlemen often doubling as moneylenders, leaving the tenant farmers to pay for everything else while facing the constant threat of eviction.

But we were also the land of Mahatma Gandhi and for twenty years Vinobha Bhave, a frail old man who had been one of Gandhi's closest associates, toured independent India urging landlords to donate land to the poor, reminding us that only the redistribution of land could give India's millions of landless labourers and tenant farmers a stake in the country's future.

Indeed, as early as 1951 Prime Minister Nehru's Government had passed a resolution limiting the amount of land any individual could own. Farmers had to 'personally' cultivate their fields and 'accept the whole risk' of cultivation. Excess land would be bought by the Government and sold cheap to tenant farmers, who would form co-operatives to prevent fragmentation.

The resolution succeeded in redistributing feudal holdings – but not to debt-laden migrant workers or subsistence farmers. It was the moderately prosperous farmer and the ubiquitous money-lender, claiming that he underwrote 'the whole risk' of farming, who had the money to take advantage of the reforms – and of all the resources the Government was pumping into the countryside.

As Mahatma Gandhi said, we should have studied our villages. But our city-bred planners did not do so. Now, instead of being exploited by large landlords, our landless labourers were being exploited by small landlords, their condition deteriorating as the price of farming increased.

By the seventies urban India learnt its errors. Rural India had become politically conscious.

In 1979 one million farmers marched on Delhi. Peasants from the north with rough blankets thrown over their shoulders. Sikh farmers on shiny tractors from what was being called the bread-basket of the Punjab. Men with turbans and elaborate ear-rings from the harsh semi-desert lands of Rajasthan; men wearing dhotis from the east; men with caste marks on their foreheads from the south. Water was their first demand. Then, seeds, fertilizers, electricity.

By 1980 the farmers weren't bothering to march on Delhi. They had launched nation-wide movements, demanding higher prices for their crops. Our intimidated leaders responded by hastily borrowing money abroad so they could give tax concessions to the farmers. Then they borrowed more money to keep the cost of food low so the poor could eat. As populism took precedence over pragmatism subsidies spiralled until the annual cost to the nation for subsidized fertilizers alone had jumped to over two billion dollars.

And like her landless labourers India was herself now in bondage, facing ever-larger interest payments to her foreign creditors on ever-larger loans.

But her poorest peasants, her migrant workers, her craftsmen dependent on diminishing village patronage, were still leaving the land.

For years we in the cities had thought that the

excitements of metropolitan life projected in glorious colour through films and television were causing the rural migration. Too late we recognized that a neglected agricultural infrastructure was sending the dispossessed into town in search of work.

When I was a child, only fifty million Indians lived in the Indian cities. Today four hundred million do, twice the population of the United States. Their numbers are threatening our urban infrastructure, and our bursting cities cannot contain them.

As our cities explode into the countryside, it is at last the turn of the peasant to patronize the urban Indian.

'For fifty years I worked this land,' an old farmer remarked when the city of Delhi reached his mud hut and prospective real-estate buyers descended on him, offering large sums of money for his unirrigated field.

'From before sunrise until after sunset I pulled the plough with my own shoulders because I didn't have enough money for a buffalo to till my field. I prayed for rain when the seeds were sown. I prayed for no rain when the plants were high. My wife collected cow dung for cooking fuel and on good years we bartered our wheat at the price set by middlemen so that we could send at least one son to school.'

He sighed with pleasure. 'Isn't it wonderful? I worked so hard for so many years but the land gave me so little. Now I get up every morning and just smile at my field. And each day I get richer.'

Eight

New Money

Anyone who doubts that India is changing should cast a quick glance around our cities, home to our new and booming urban middle class.

Whole families dressed in shiny synthetic fabrics squash onto scooters driven by men with pomaded hair wearing shades and terylene trousers and those pointed shoes that used to be called brothel-creepers.

Higher up the feeding-chain there are gold watches, German cars, Italian clothes, yachts and airplanes, Cristal and Dom Perignon champagnes, reserved tables for sprawling families in the most expensive restaurants and discothèques. An awful lot of caviare congealing uneaten in an awful lot of Lalique bowls signals the new Indian attitude: if you've got it, flaunt it.

In the old days, if you had it, you hid it. We were a poor country and self-denial was solidarity.

I remember when we were undergraduates at Cambridge University we were allowed only the bare minimum of hard currency to cover our fees. But we didn't mind too much. We were still under the sway of Mahatma

Gandhi's austerity – although Sarojini Naidu, the indomitable woman who was Gandhi's companion in so many of the great non-violent adventures which ended the British Raj, had once observed that it cost Indians a lot to keep Gandhi poor.

Twenty years later we would understand Sarojini Naidu's perspicacious comment when our economy remained stuck at the dismal low dismissed disparagingly by our economists as the Hindu rate of growth. Then we would admit that the austerities enforced on us by the errors of central planning had proved even more expensive for the nation than Mahatma Gandhi's poverty.

But in the early sixties we seemed to have got our planning right. Analysts around the world were telling us that India was ready for economic take-off, and as undergraduates we could still afford to feel morally superior to the self-indulgences of our colleagues – especially our subcontinental colleagues at Cambridge.

But then reverse snobbery was our only option when the Pakistan Government had no currency restrictions and the richest Pakistani students could show off their wealth. Oh those wicked Pakistanis, so stylishly dressed by Anderson and Shepherd. Our penury limited us to a determined display of homespun modesty rather than dashing wardrobes from the most expensive Savile Row tailors. How else were we to make a virtue of our poverty except by adopting a stern Robespierran disdain for the Danton-like sybarites from north of the subcontinental border?

They kept polo ponies. They smoked Havana cigars. They raced around in Lotus sports cars with headlights that went up and down like eyes winking invitingly, and a lot of pretty European girls learning English in local language-schools took up those invitations, a lot more than ever accepted invitations from the impoverished Indian students.

Still, we did have one thing the flashy Pakistani students lacked. The Prime Minister of India was an Honorary Doctor of Cambridge University. Because of Nehru we affected contempt for what India's planners called 'luxury goods'. We would eschew luxury goods for cheap goods which we could make ourselves. We would nationalize a lot of our industries. We would regulate what was left.

We would ignore the alarmed voices raised in India's Parliament against this ideological posturing. 'A country that loses sixty per cent of its water every year through mismanagement cannot afford ideology,' those voices thundered. But we were living in the age of ideology, the very heart of a Cold War that pitted social justice against ruthless capitalism, and we wore our poverty with pride.

After all, it was the heyday of Nehru's socialism. He had been honoured by one of the most respected academies in the world. And he was One of Us.

Free of such enervating considerations, the Pakistani students continued to holiday on the French Riviera, driving from one modish resort to another. Our crushing exchange restrictions meant that we couldn't go away unless we were prepared to spend days standing by the side of highways with our thumbs tentatively extended, unconvincing hitch-hikers.

Perhaps such humiliations led one of those impoverished Indian students, Rajiv Gandhi, to begin lifting currency restrictions when he became Prime Minister. Or perhaps it was a reaction to the accumulation of further restrictions imposed on the country by his mother.

Prime Minister Indira Gandhi had spent most of the

seventies expanding government until it interfered in every aspect of Indian life. During her time in office the steep rise in world oil prices had sent the cost of essential commodities in India soaring. Workers in the nationalized industries were striking for higher wages, rural India was demanding a larger share of resources.

But Mrs Gandhi proceeded to nationalize insurance companies and banks. And her new restraints on private industry became so elaborate they assured a virtual monopoly to anyone who succeeded in actually obtaining an industrial licence, even though the successful industrialist was still not allowed to produce to full capacity, only to a government quota. If the quota was too small and demand too great, black-marketeering filled the void, creating mountains of undeclared cash that could not be used to build more factories, grow more food, create more jobs.

An awed report in the *Economist* noted of our system, 'This has no equal in the world. In many ways it puts Soviet central planning to shame.'

Less charitably, our own economists said we had created the Land of the Permit Licence Raj.

It was all done for the best possible motives: self-reliance, independence from the western commercial imperialism that had replaced western political imperialism.

But even when we were undergraduates, secretly envying our Pakistani colleagues, we suspected that something had gone wrong.

Still, it's never too late to right a wrong and one of our contemporaries was finally doing something about it.

Dismissing our hollow self-reliance, Rajiv Gandhi was

opening India's economy to the world, deregulating industry, slashing taxes.

What's more, he was taking a visible delight in those sinful imported items we had been denied so long. Like the Indian housewife in V. S. Naipaul's *Area of Darkness*, our new Prime Minister was 'craze for foreign. Just craze for foreign.'

He wore imported aviator glasses and drove imported fast cars and drank imported mineral water. Where Nehru and Shashtri had travelled by commercial airlines, he was having a whole Boeing reappointed for his use, while the decorators who refurbished his home were themselves being decorated with government honours.

Watching him we realized that Homespun was Out, Luxury Goods were In.

After forty long years we could say goodbye to the hair-shirt of poverty.

For the first time in independent India it was politically correct to be rich.

Nine

An Embarrassment of Riches

Delhi is among the fastest-growing cities in the world but I think the census-takers start their counting in the winter time when the city is overrun by hordes of Westerners fleeing the snow.

The foreigners who arrived in Delhi during the seventies came in search of spiritual enlightenment. Now it was the glorious eighties, and our Prime Minister, Rajiv Gandhi, was a young, good-looking baby-boomer who was liberalizing the Indian economy. Money had become the new enlightenment.

So I wasn't surprised when a gentleman approached me at a dinner party.

'Five hundred international Young Presidents and their wives are arriving for India 1986. We would like you to address them, give them a different picture of India that will encourage investment.'

I looked solemn. The gravity of his demeanour suggested the approach of – well, what was a Young President?

'Financial and industrial dynamos. They all became heads of their own companies by the age of forty.'

And what was India 1986?

'An attempt to get them to start companies here. The other speakers are Dr Kissinger, Mother Teresa and the Dalai Lama.'

This was serious flattery – to be told your peers are a Star, a Saint and a God. Mere patriotism paled into insignificance. But what do you say to Young Presidents when you have neither expertise nor sanctity on your side, and certainly not divinity? I had a few jokes. Was that enough to make these tigers of trade invest in India?

I rang Headquarters, Young Presidents' Organization, New York. Brisk voices replied, conjuring up images of smart young things in uniforms pushing flagged figures of entrepreneurs around a map of the world.

'I don't want to come on after Mother Teresa,' I said, appealing to their distant sympathy.

'Why not?'

'Nobody can follow Mother Teresa. It's like coming on after Little Richard.'

'Oh, really? We'll fix it. Our literature is on its way. Have a good day.'

The literature arrived, a curriculum appropriately bound in that luxurious crimson associated with Les Must de Cartier. Within it were photographs of a large number of speakers, and Dr Kissinger and the Dalai Lama weren't among them. I had been conned by a Young President.

But my disappointment dissolved in the anticipation of hearing Ms Bettina Arndt address five hundred corporate presidents on the theme *Not Tonight, Dear, I have a Headache*, followed, perhaps too obviously, by *Is the Boss a Lousy Lover?*

Boy, that should pull a lot of investment for India.

Sandwiched between the editor of the *Washington Times's* lecture on *South Africa: Race War or Modus Vivendi* and the Porsche chairman's lecture on *Planning an International Business in Uncertain Times*, someone was going to discuss the dilemma of 'plateau-ing'.

Plateau-ing?

Whatever plateau-ing meant, it was going to be discussed in the lecture *Resolving the Mid-Life Crisis: Insights From India*. Could the speaker pull it off, I wondered. Mid-day Crises we could do in India, even Mid-Week Crises. But had we clambered sufficiently high up the evolutionary ladder to qualify for Mid-Life Crises?

And my own lecture on the Westerners who had given up their expensive toys in the hope of acquiring India's fabled spiritual depth, while Indians traded anything they had, including spiritual depth, for the chance of owning those discarded toys – was it an illustration of such crisis?

By the time the conference was to begin the Prime Minister of India, our Foreign Secretary, our top advisers on Planning and Administrative reforms were all on the agenda. A weight lifted from my shoulders. If they couldn't convince the entrepreneurs of the world to invest in India, who could? Unless the way to a president's heart was through his stomach, in which case we had as back-up the five primary sauces of India, to be demonstrated in a lecture on *The Colourful World of Indian Cuisine: Brown, Red, Yellow, White and Green*.

And then the five hundred presidents and their wives were in town, snarling up the traffic, hogging the hotel rooms. Business as usual.

Not so usual were the side-shows in the hotel foyers in homage to the one essential required for inclusion in the

Young Presidents' Association – Big Bucks. Jewellers bent over gems, peering through the loupes fixed to their eyes. Vendors who had come all the way from Benares smiled politely as they tried to slide fragile glass bangles over wrists larger than any they had ever seen. Veiled women from Rajasthan leaned over copper bowls filled with henna paste to paint elaborate fertility designs on the palms of queuing wives. Sometimes the ladies were joined by the Young Presidents themselves, but no one laughed during the conference when men proffered hands covered with female fertility designs. After all, the rich are supposed to be different.

The only person who hadn't grasped this was an astrologer seated like a pasha on cushions, surrounded by adoring Westerners as he ministered to future mid-life crises.

I watched a personable young fruit and vegetable millionaire from Australia have his future told. He was surprised by the astrologer's accurate reading of his past, thrilled to learn that he hadn't yet plateau-ed.

'But greater success is yet to come,' the soothsayer shouted in delight, staring at the horoscope he had cast. 'You will change direction into new paths of great wealth. More remunerative than your present business even.'

'What will I be doing?' the Australian millionaire enquired eagerly.

'Have no fears, sir. Soon you will become a, a . . .'

Twenty of us waited, holding our breath.

'A money-lender!' the astrologer announced triumphantly, dismissing fruit and vegetable fortunes as slim pickings compared to the wealth to be had from loan-sharking, which lifted a man into the rarefied world inhabited by the truly rich.

Actually what identified these rich was their sheer stamina. From dawn jogging and yoga classes via a quick swim and a set of tennis, they raced off to learn how to tie saris and turbans, drove a hundred miles to Agra to see the Taj Mahal, bought carpets, were received for tea by a real president – the President of India – watched polo matches played by the Sixty-First Cavalry Regiment, visited outlying factories and villages, dined in different houses to see how real Indians lived, shopped ceaselessly, and still managed to attend the lectures taking place throughout the day. And they were only in town for a week.

The crisp voices from New York, in person belonging to people more *Cosmopolitan* than Third Reich, remained maddeningly unflappable as they orchestrated solutions to all this busy work and other India '86 problems. I complained that now I was following not only Mother Teresa but the Prime Minister as well. What kind of billing was that? They clucked sympathetically, didn't change a thing, and gave me a sandalwood medallion engraved with my name and designation – Faculty – and a cloth satchel filled with that glossy paper that sticks to your fingers. More crimson brochures which listed the best eating and shopping in India, proliferating proof of the twentieth century's drive to consume.

At least that's what Mother Teresa implied in her shockingly contemporary appeal. She wanted help for victims of AIDS. The Young Presidents had already agreed to ante-up a million tax-deductible dollars for her hospices in New York. Now she was telling them their money wasn't good enough. She wanted their personal participation, volunteers to work with the patients. The haze of sentimentality evaporated instantly. No one was prepared to extend a

hennaed hand in lieu of a cheque book. Easier to accommodate was her request that they be humane to their
employees – enquire about their children's names.

The Young Presidents knew what to call each other.
Apart from the sandalwood medallions hanging around
their necks there was a crimson book titled *Who's Here*
giving their names, and then their nicknames.

Wiping tears of emotion from their eyes as Mother
Teresa ended her address the Eds, Bobs, Als, Chucks,
married to the Babses, Frans, Connies, Sues, settled back
in their chairs to listen to the next speaker – a man who
could have been one of their own.

Head of a country by the age of forty, it was the open-
minded Prime Minister of India telling them how he
wanted to take his unwieldy corporation into the twenty-
first century. Just as Mother Teresa was the acceptable
face of charity, so Rajiv Gandhi was the acceptable face
of Third World leadership.

When he had left everyone filled in their evaluation
forms. There were six categories and eight sub-categories
by which all speakers – saints, Prime Ministers, geo-
political experts – were to be judged. One was the lowest
rating, Ten the highest. Rajiv Gandhi only made Sixes and
Sevens. Mother Teresa was a straight and unanimous Ten.
After all, she was a star.

And stars are for consumers. As Mother Teresa tried to
make her get-away she was hauled out of her van by
millionaires pleading to be photographed with her.
Looking like an irritated ET in her white sari with its blue
border she reluctantly dismounted from her van again and
again. But she was consoled when she heard her score.

'I'm a Ten! I'm a Ten!' she crowed to her nuns. 'What
does that mean?'

'You're the new Bo Derek!' said friends who had worked with her from the time she had begun her mission. The younger nuns, just in from the world, giggled knowingly when the friends promised to bring her a video of the movie so she could see what a Ten really was.

Things are seldom what they seem. These movers and shakers from the West who were devouring India like Great White sharks also had another persona, one capable of delving deeper into the subcontinent. At the end of every lecture they asked highly informed questions about Indian political and economic matters. When had they found the time to think about such things? That whole week, in crowded conference halls, global info-babble had seeped from under closed doors. To be a dynamo in today's world did you need a capacity to simply absorb information like a human floppy disk in order to generate wealth?

It was a mystery. Almost as mysterious as the closing spectacular of India '86. Destination Secret, said the invitation. Black Tie. And the next day they would all be gone.

Young millionaires who had brought canned food against India's many diseases distributed it to the surprised Delhi University students who had been their guides. Then the turban and sari experts arrived. For two hours turbans were wound onto the heads of the presidents, saris pleated around the waists of the more daring ladies. Clapping enthusiastically at their costumes they made their way to the hotel foyer in anticipation of Destination Secret.

Suddenly a fanfare of trumpets cleared a path through one thousand cheering guests. Nodding graciously, a clutch of India's ex-rulers dressed in royal garb made their way through the crowd and down the marble hotel steps to mount the vintage Bentleys and Rolls-Royces lined up behind the horse carriages and caparisoned elephants that were to lead the procession to Destination Secret.

The millionaires joined the procession, clambering into palanquins borne by liveried bearers, or onto camels, or horses. Or they walked so that they could better enjoy the spectacle of the avenue guarded by Gurkha soldiers standing in front of the hundreds of cummerbunded torch-bearers holding lanterns. Thus, piped by Indian wedding bands, watched by gawping Indians, we sashayed out of the front gates of the hotel to Destination Secret – which turned out to be the back gate of the same hotel.

Lining the approach to the back gate were mounted Lancers. Beautiful young girls dressed in traditional red and ochre long skirts were flinging jasmine garlands at the ladies, marking the foreheads of the presidents with red powder and spraying everyone in sight with scented rose water. To our left, a full military band, white uniforms bright against the dark lawns, was playing viceregal tunes as the ex-royals preceded the entrepreneurs into a Moghul tent for champagne cocktails. It was a fabulous finale. Every element of India – Moghul Empire, British Raj, traditional Hindu, contemporary wedding, erstwhile Maharajah, rather like the five primary sauces of Indian cuisine – had been reproduced to please the jaded palates of the Young Presidents. And perhaps attract investment.

The banging of an enormous brass gong, followed by the cries of 'Hoshiar! Hoshiar!' once used by eunuchs to inform the harem that the ruler approached, alerted us to drain our champagne glasses and follow the Maharajahs into the banquet hall.

Over dinner our silver platters were constantly replenished with kebabs, curries, Indian breads, vegetables; our glasses filled to the brim with wines, champagnes, liqueurs to keep us busy until the band came on.

Then for four hours an Indian dance band played the kind of music the Young Presidents must have loved, because the crowded dance floor couldn't take any more financial dynamos and they were jiving in the aisles.

The gentleman on my left, a cabinet minister from the Royal Thai Government, observed laconically that just that morning he had been addressing these demon dancers on the issue of Population Control in the Third World.

'By the way, do you have a key chain?' he asked. As I rummaged in my handbag I could hear one of the Young Presidents on the microphone crooning *Feelings* to his applauding colleagues.

'Sorry. I'm not carrying any keys.'

The cabinet minister reached into his elegantly cut dinner jacket and produced one. I examined it. There was a plastic bubble in the centre of the key chain. Over the bubble was printed the instruction, *In Case of Emergency Break Glass*. The minister lifted a candle so I could see more clearly. Under the bubble was – an electric blue condom.

Someone pulled me from my chair to join the singers. Was this an emergency? Would an electric blue condom help? Or should I save my key chain in case I was invited to address next year's conference?

India '86 was already over. On the dance floor they were holding hands and singing the theme song of the African famine, *We Are the World, We Are the People*.

According to the brochure of the Young Presidents' Organization, 'If you liked the movie *Out of Africa* you are going to love Africa '87.'

Ten

Typing

'It's a scandal!' the French intellectual said with a passion available only to energetic Westerners. I looked around the bazaar nervously and saw small boys in torn short pants kicking flimsy plastic shopping-bags across a dirty courtyard.

The year was 1996, and we were in one of those shopping complexes which have burgeoned all over the major Indian cities – hideous structures made of unpainted concrete, red streaks of betel-juice marking their chipped steps.

The stench of badly cured leather competed with the smell of fast food being fried in corner cafés where customers had stopped for snacks after renting their evening's entertainment from video shops. Racks of garments collected dust in crowded corridors next to rows of shoes piled in precarious pyramids that could not be crammed into the tiny shops. Loud film music emanated from record stores, drowning civilized conversation, disturbing the students pounding away at their rented keyboards in their

Computer Course schools consisting of two tables, two chairs, two machines.

'What is a scandal?' In the presence of so many possibilities I was unable to identify the target of her anger.

'These videos!' she hissed, waving at the garish poster of an Indian film taped to the window of a store. I examined the poster. It had a certain vitality, putting me in mind of the Indian hotel that advertised a stripper's attractions with the headline *Come· and See. Crude and Vivacious Gwendolina.* Surely even a French intellectual was not going to demand aesthetics in an Indian bazaar?

'Do you know what these video people are doing?' she persisted angrily, and I felt something bad was coming. 'They have put religious rituals on film! Imagine switching on a machine so that your priest can chant prayers while you prostrate yourself in front of the television!'

I stared at her in blank relief. She waved an embroidered muslin sleeve at me, outraged at my obstinate stupidity. 'But just think. People are *worshipping* their videos!'

What's the big deal? I thought to myself. Worshipping videos? Get a grip. This is India. We worship air-conditioners and computers and cash registers and bullock carts – in an annual ritual called Weapon Worship.

For millennia Indians have believed man is distinguished from his fellow animals by his capacity to make tools. By honouring our implements we honour human ingenuity, and Weapon Worship originated with warriors honouring their weapons, the tools of their trade. In modern India people still place garlands on the machines of their differing trades, hoping for an auspicious response. Actually, any response at all will do, so on the day of Weapon Worship machines are offered coconuts, smeared with vermilion, propitiated by so many sticks of incense that they disappear into clouds of scented smoke.

In our electronic age new machines are arriving with such velocity that honouring them can take more than just a day. Only a handful of years ago we were not allowed to import colour television sets. Today colour televisions are made in the country. Indian-made computers, fax machines, telephone answering machines and all the other paraphernalia of instant communications are making it possible for Indians to be part of the future.

A few years ago our telephone system could only be described as disastrous, available just in cities to people prepared to queue for years or pay hefty bribes. Now public telephones in the countryside are freeing the farmer from the scourge of rapacious middlemen, enabling him to establish the market price of his crops himself.

The hand-held cellular telephone, that appendage of the successful urbanite, has even made its entry into parts of rural India. Sometimes you can see outside his mud and stone house a villager lying on his perennial string bed, a bullock or two tethered in the background, near an Indian car parked under the shade of a tree. The farmer himself will be drawing on his hookah and talking into a cellular telephone, possibly making a real-estate deal as the city's boundaries stretch towards his fields. Or he may be establishing crop prices from the grain market. Or he may be hiring an Indian-made tractor.

The surging energy gathering momentum in India is visible on our crowded city streets. When did so many Indians buy those cars which they drive so dangerously, and those awful car horns which they lean on from the moment they switch on the ignition? What are all those Benetton shops doing next to those sari shops, those

Coca-Cola ads next to those ads for freeze-dried spices? Are those Cybercafés opening next to kebab restaurants? Is this the conspicuous consumption which we have so long abhorred? Or is this the new India framed by the old India, determined to take advantage of the breaks that are coming its way?

Those breaks took a long time coming, stifled by decades of steady encroachment by the state, until an economic impasse in the nineties forced the reforms which are finally releasing India's immense commercial energies. You have only to turn on Indian-made television to see the huge increase in goods now available to the Indian consumer, only to open the morning newspaper in any Indian city to see how many foreign investors are prepared to grapple with India's byzantine rules to get their feet on the first rung of the ladder of her impending economic boom.

Once it was the dream of educated Indians to be hired by government – government jobs meant a steady income and no one was ever fired. The dreams are changing. A feeling is in the air; government jobs are going to get leaner and less secure, while the private sector is expanding and paying higher salaries.

There used to be a joke about the state of Kerala, which produces a vast number of government clerks because it has the highest literacy rate in the country. Its politically conscious population are often communists.

So someone asks a person from Kerala, 'Are you a capitalist or a Marxist?'

'I'm a typist,' he replies.

No one wants to be a typist any more. The ugly Indian shopping complexes were once crammed with one-room typing schools. Now they are bursting with computer schools, evidence of the hunger for learning improvement that typify the Indian.

Indians are nothing if not canny. They can s the wind is now blowing from another directi there's money to be had in the change.

Five years ago only five thousand Indians were working in computers. Today a quarter of a million Indians are busy producing computer software which is used around the world, bought by the Fortune Five Hundred Companies. Tomorrow electronics might well employ five hundred thousand people – our youngest industry is also among our fastest growing, already exporting a billion dollars' worth of electronic goods abroad every year.

It has been said that what his Western counterpart demands as a right is seen by the Indian as an opportunity. And for nearly two centuries we have known that opportunity and communications are inseparable. Communications conquered us – the telegraph, the train, the constantly communicating bureaucracy of the British Raj. We were avid to own it, and, when the British left, from four major universities the number of Indian universities jumped to over ninety. The average number of students at each university grew until today our largest universities, in Calcutta and Delhi, Madras and Bombay, have over a hundred thousand students, and annually turn away twice that number in applicants. Five million Indians graduate from university each year, and technological training institutes generate a steady stream of scientists and engineers.

Yet too many Indians still cannot read a name or write a number, a huge brake on our hopes of future development. Today over ninety per cent of South Koreans are fully literate, but fifty per cent of Indians are illiterate – a result of Prime Minister Nehru's concentration on higher education, and the Third Five-Year Plan, under Indira Gandhi, which did not give literacy high priority, although literacy produces a rise in the standard of living and a corresponding plunge in population.

To the great relief of the poor, primary education has finally become our top planning priority. Poverty is a state of mind as well as an economic condition, a hopelessness, a knowledge that things can never change. Any chink in that bleak wall of despair, and the poor are the first to race through it. For them it is a matter of life or death. Ask any Indian villager what he wants and the reply is always, an education for my children. Ask any indigent Indian living in a town or city what he wants and the answer is invariably the same.

Those who are not so poor share the same passion. Today the pressure on school and university places is such that children as young as three years old have to take an examination before they can even get into nursery schools. Lamp-posts and trees in Indian towns carry advertisements from people offering themselves as tutors to school or college students. Parents are prepared to pay huge sums of money known as capitation fees, but which are actually bribes by a prettier name, to guarantee their children a place in private schools and colleges. I once met the president of America's most prestigious business school, who had been to India on a holiday. He was overwhelmed by the number of Indian parents who located him in his various hotel suites, demanding, begging, pleading for their children's admission.

The skills of the modern world are by no means alien to us. Doctors, engineers, laboratory workers, economists, accountants – at the level of medium technology, Indians are second to none. And each time there is a new advance in technology, Indians are ready to seize it.

And when Silicon Valley in California sleeps, Indian scientists wake up in what is being called the Silicon Valley of Asia, the Indian city of Bangalore, to address the same problems that their sleeping American colleagues tried to solve the previous day, taking advantage of the electronic phenomenon which enables knowledge to be exchanged on a twenty-four-hour basis on the information super-highway.

Some might ask why there isn't a bigger brain-drain from India today. Many Indian scientists reply that they do not want to lose a world of close family relationships and festivals – where religious ceremonies can safely be transferred onto videotape. Where newspapers, describing the popularity of televised mythologies, can safely carry the headline *Gods Work*.

Ancient pragmatisms are India's saving grace, preserving a way of life in which the machine is still used by man, not one in which man becomes his machine. But that is a difficult thing to explain to someone from the West. Which is why the angry French intellectual saw electronic worship as a scandal and I saw it as a celebration.

For me the real scandal was that four hundred million Indians still had no machines to worship.

Eleven

Dreaming

It is so dispiriting to be an Indian reading about Malaysia, South Korea, Singapore, Thailand, Indonesia. With their booming economies our neighbours are called the South East Asian Tigers. To my chagrin India is usually described by analysts around the world as the Caged Tiger, a country that has yet to exploit its enormous potential.

And then I read these comparisons between India and China. India is always the elephant, China the hare.

And then a banker rings me from London. He is analysing the Indian market.

'Is it true that India has twenty million dollar millionaires?' he asks reverently.

The meter ticks expensively as the banker and myself silently consider the implications of the question. Twenty million of us? Dollar millionaires? Could such a thing be possible? Who are these millionaires anyway? How did they make their money?

I guess some got rich from the flourishing black-market our government controls created by 'protecting the poor'.

Some were the kings of the Permit Licence Raj, who

monopolized the very industries government restrictions were designed to prevent them from monopolizing.

Some were stockbrokers who inflated the markets out of all proportion because too many industries were nationalized, leaving too much cash chasing too few company shares.

Some owed their wealth to the value of their houses in the bursting and ill-planned Indian metropolises, where real estate today is more expensive than in New York or London.

And many, far too many, had once been poor politicians and bureaucrats.

But the poorest Indian is still poorer than his counterpart in sub-Saharan Africa. It should not be so. With our thrift as a people, our technical manpower, our stable administration, we had the resources to become an economic tiger long ago. Alas, busy drawing maps for our lives with the same high-handedness with which nineteenth-century Europe had once drawn maps of our geography, our political leaders had ensured that a country with four times the population of America was producing the same amount of goods as Holland.

They need only have looked around the world to see the obvious. Outside the restrictions of their own country, Indians who live abroad are a blur of economic activity. Why can't we do the same at home? Why can't we produce more than Holland?

But one Indian prime minister after another, in the attempt to remove poverty, had only mired us further in poverty.

In the fifties Nehru had dreamt of a self-sufficient economy through rapid industrialization and neglected the needs of rural India.

The gains of the Green Revolution of the sixties were lost in the seventies to obsessive centralization and spiralling farm subsidies.

In the eighties, Rajiv Gandhi's interest in a new India was soon exchanged for the political manoeuvrings of the old India, while his successor, V. P. Singh, was less concerned with economic development than with political change.

By the nineties it was too late to ignore the economy. We had never defaulted on our debts. Now our foreign currency reserves were so depleted the nation's gold was sent to London as surety against international loans. The world's credit agencies immediately demanded that India reduce her public sector, cut subsidies to agriculture, reform the tax structure.

In 1991 Prime Minister Rao undertook the delicate balancing act of moving the creaking machinery of Indian socialism towards a market economy.

Now India stands on the brink of a new millennium, and Growth and Opportunity have become the new Indian slogans. Can they bend the bars that keep India caged? Can we sprint past China's hare?

Look at what we have going for us. Two hundred and fifty million Indians are part of a still growing middle class. On top of that, four hundred million Indians can purchase essentials. That's an awful lot of clothes and cooking utensils. With our creeping rate of growth we already possess a market-place of half a billion people. Increase it and we could double our middle class, make it possible for every Indian to purchase essentials. Then we would have a market-place of nearly a billion people, and from twenty million dollar millionaires today we could have ten times that number tomorrow. Two hundred million dollar millionaires. More than in the United States. In fact, nearly as many dollar millionaires as there are Americans.

There is really nothing to stop us. Unless political opportunism, the dread mistress of Indian economics, exacts her usual price.

But democracy is a time bomb and we are the largest democracy in the world. We are also, as the writer V. S. Naipaul said, the land of a million mutinies now.

Twelve

Writing

In the 1890s, when the terrible cruelty of the caste system was still denying education to millions of Indians, the ruler of Baroda, one of India's largest kingdoms, made education free for all castes.

In ancient India castes had once been like guilds, merely describing a man's occupation. Though belonging to the lowest caste, the sage Vyasa had compiled India's epic religious poem, *The Mahabharata*, while the son of a low-caste woman had created the glorious Maurya Empire. Indeed, when his grandson, the Emperor Asoka, converted to Buddhism, Asoka's great universities had disseminated the Buddha's teachings until they became the religion of Asia.

But over millennia caste somehow degenerated until a man's occupation became an immutable fact of birth. The lowest caste of scavengers and refuse collectors were treated as anathema, polluting other castes by their very shadows. They were called untouchables.

Death was the sentence for an untouchable who wanted an education. The Laws of Manu, followed by orthodox

Hindus, prescribed the method. If an untouchable even overheard Sanskrit, the language of the scriptures, he was to be killed by having molten lead poured into his ears.

In Baroda, allowed education at last, a young untouchable boy studied so hard that he was able to acquire a Bachelor of Arts degree from Bombay University. Then he got a scholarship to Columbia University in New York. Leaving the United States as a Doctor of Philosophy, he went on to London University and gained a Doctor of Science degree.

Twice over the untouchable boy achieved the impossible. He became Dr Ambedkar.

Back in India Mahatma Gandhi was insisting that untouchables be called Harijans – children of god. But Dr Ambedkar knew that an untouchable by any other name was still the detritus of a religion, the living hell from which Hindus hoped to liberate themselves through good acts to be acknowledged in rebirths higher up the ladder of reincarnation.

Determined to change a vast continent where nearly one third of the population was exploited by caste discrimination he took another degree in London, this time in law.

In 1946 a committee was formed to write India's constitution, and by 1947 Dr Ambedkar was its chairman.

During the four long years it took to draft the Indian constitution, the subcontinent was convulsed by change. The British were departing. Five hundred independent rulers were merging their kingdoms into India and Pakistan, the East and West halves of Pakistan separated from each other by a thousand miles of India. The day after the two new nations of India and Pakistan became free, Britain announced its dreaded partition awards and the subcontinent erupted in carnage as Hindus, Muslims, and Sikhs fled their ancestral homes in one of the largest migrations in human history that would, in a single year, leave one million dead, over seven million homeless.

And through all this raging turbulence, work on the Indian constitution continued.

To assist him in drafting the constitution Dr Ambedkar had at his disposal not just the constitutions of the western world, but ancient India's great work on the science of government – the *Artha Shastra*, attributed to Kautilya, a minister in the court of the Maurya Empire.

He also had at his disposal history.

On the third and final reading of the Bill to enact the Indian constitution into law Dr Ambedkar noted.

'It is not that India did not know what Democracy is. There was a time when India was studded with republics.

'It is not that India did not know Parliaments or Parliamentary Procedure. The Sanghas [Buddhist monastic orders] had rules regarding seating arrangements, rules regarding Motions, Resolutions, Quorum, Whips, Counting of Votes, Voting by Ballot, Censure Motion, Regularization, *Res Judicata*, etc. . . . borrowed from the Political Assemblies functioning in the country at the time.

'This democratic system India lost. Will she lose it a second time?

'If we wish to maintain democracy not merely in form but also in fact . . . we must observe the caution which John Stuart Mill has given all those who are interested in the maintenance of democracy: namely, not to lay their liberties at the feet of even a great man, or to trust him with powers which enable him to subvert their institutions.

'Hero-worship is a sure road to degradation and to eventual dictatorship.'

The Sovereign Republic of India was formally proclaimed on January 26, 1950, governed by a constitution which guaranteed

> The State shall not deny to any person equality before the law
> The State shall not discriminate against any citizen on grounds of religion, race, caste, sex
> 'Untouchability' is abolished and its practice in any form is forbidden.

Now India prepared to go to the polls for her first general election.

On that great occasion the untouchable lawyer who had drafted her constitution reminded the people of India that it was only a piece of paper until it was inscribed on the hearts of its citizens.

Thirteen

The Voice of the People

For sheer idiosyncratic panache the spectacle of Indian democracy is unique. Where else would a hundred thousand naked sadhus with matted hair break off their meditations and descend from their mountain caves to scale the towering gates of the Indian Parliament – locked for the first time against a squirming wall of holy men waving iron tridents, determined to breach the nation's citadel and ban cow slaughter.

Where else would a mass of hermaphrodites and eunuchs, dressed in brilliantly coloured saris and weighted down by jewels, march on the capital to demonstrate against Family Planning – on the grounds that it would statistically lessen their odds of being born.

Such displays suggest that the concept of nationhood which we took so unthinkingly from nineteenth-century Europe is too constricting for our diversity. But half a century after we ceased to be a colony we still bristle with the over-sensitive antennae of a colonized people, vainly struggling to become a European nation state.

And Indian politicians assume that, individually, they

alone can define such a nation state because only they know the 'true Indian masses'. Fortunately, the true Indian masses enjoy proving otherwise – a discovery made by our first Prime Minister when he toured the tribal areas of North-East India.

The tribal populations of the hill tracts of the Indian north-east often demonstrate against the cutting down of their forests by lumber contractors who contribute heavily to political coffers. Yet any tribal who goes to Delhi to plead the tribal cause ends up in what the Prime Minister of India believes to be the zenith of tribal ambition – a photo-opportunity with the nation's leader wearing some strange tribal head-dress in jaunty solidarity.

So a number of press photographers were accompanying Prime Minister Nehru when he made a much publicized visit to their hill tracts in 1957. As the airplane circled the valley, between the beautiful but increasingly denuded wooded hills, several hundred tiny figures could be seen waiting – tribals who had journeyed from their inaccessible homelands to greet the Indian Prime Minister.

There were chiefs with huge head-dresses of feathers and beads and horns, like dignified lines of eastern Montezumas. Young women with long black hair cascading over their backs. Tribal matrons in woven shawls and sarongs. Handsome younger men with smooth, hairless faces and elegantly slanted eyes, lithe bodies visible under the stiff tribal cloths that covered one muscled shoulder, leaving bare the other shoulder to handle a spear or a bow.

The airplane landed, a great white bird with the symbol of the Indian nation, Emperor Asoka's pillar of truth, blazoned on its side. Would the child-like tribals be frightened by this miracle of aerodynamics descending from the heavens with its cargo of democratic divinity? Would they run for cover? But no, they were standing steady under quivering head-dresses watching aircraft personnel leaping out to fix the steps for the Prime Minister's descent, as the press photographers pushed forward for a clear view through their lenses.

Finally the great man himself appeared – to be received by a reverence so profound that even the accompanying journalists were silenced. Possessing a sense of history, the leader solemnly descended the aircraft steps, assuming this warlike people wished to give him a colourful guard of honour.

I suppose they did. Because as soon as he was on terra firma, they all turned with regimental precision and lifted their colourful sarongs. The Prime Minister of India found himself taking the salute of hundreds of naked tribal behinds.

Fourteen

Management Crisis

Modern India is a fiction.

A fiction in search of an administration.

The visions of an older generation – freedom, equality, non-violence – have over fifty years been turned into siren songs by what the Indian writer Nirad Chaudhari called the Continent of Circe. He chose an apt name for India: her political seductions have truly made swine out of men. And women.

It's the scale of India, you see. In 1911, when George V came to Delhi for his coronation as King Emperor, even he was impressed by the magnificence of his representative. Indeed, one Viceroy of India had observed, 'The Emperor of China and I rule half the world and still have time for tea.'

Increasingly, India's political leaders are finding tea and monarchy more palatable than governance. I suppose, the reflected power of such a giant land creates megalomania in her elected representatives. Democracy may demand accountability but when you are received by crowds of half a million, it's hard to believe you are accountable to anyone.

Megalomania is also a convenient retreat from the alarming speed with which India is changing.

Partially, it is politics. Indians are no longer prepared to endure the injustices of the past. And living in a democracy they are prepared to do something about it.

Partially, it is economics. In fifty years we have not yet found a system of development that meets the needs both of our vociferous population and of a world of exploding scientific and financial expansion.

The chaos is enough to intimidate anyone. Rather than undertake the duties of their office, our leaders have too often settled for redefining the privileges of office, making political corruption so endemic that winning an election in India today is tantamount to winning a lottery for the family.

We are even pilloried by satirists for having a hereditary democracy while Britain makes do with a constitutional monarchy.

Still, from the vantage of time it is possible to see patterns leading us from the constitutional dreams of Dr Ambedkar and the incorruptible non-violent politics of Mahatma Gandhi to our present condition.

THREE

Fifteen

Last Rites

I had just turned five years old when I found myself attending my first political event. The cold January day had started normally enough. My brother and I were playing under a winter sun in the garden of our house in Delhi while our parents chose to sit on the verandah listening to the large wooden radio.

We never listened to the radio, only watched it, fascinated by the bronze netting vibrating with the resonance of the broadcast. But this afternoon my father suddenly shouted 'No!' with such force the servants came out to see what was happening. We ran to the verandah to find Mother crying. To our surprise the servants were weeping too. Over the crackle of the radio the announcer repeated that Mahatma Gandhi had been shot three times and killed.

We were so small we were not quite sure who Mahatma Gandhi was, or even whether he was human or one of India's many deities. Later we learned he had been shot by a Hindu fanatic as he was preparing to leave on a peace march for the killing fields of Partition, where millions of people, uprooted by the map-drawing of the British Empire that had given birth to the two nations of India and Pakistan only six months earlier, were still fleeing the orgy of fear and savagery that already had left a million Hindus and Muslims and Sikhs slaughtered in their wake.

After all this time I cannot remember the exact sequence of events, only that Father rushed to the house where the Mahatma had been shot. Mother, too distraught to leave home, insisted the servants take us with them to watch the Mahatma's body being taken to the funeral pyre.

Wondering what the excitement was about, we ran beside the servants towards the road where Gandhi's funeral cortège was expected. The pavements were already crowded with people standing in rows four deep. It was a most un-Indian crowd. There was no noise. Everyone had changed into white, the Indian colour of mourning that was no colour at all. There was no pushing or shoving, as if the whole city was frozen and one man's death bore evidence to the horror and the savagery that had turned a city of half a million people overnight into a city of two million as refugees poured in from the carnage of Partition.

I recall sitting on someone's shoulder, looking over the mass of heads, not scared in those crowds which newspapers with black bands to signify a nation in mourning would estimate at being a million and a half people.

In silence we watched the lorry bearing the Mahatma's body slowly approaching. It was crowded with bare-headed old people dressed in white sitting uncomfortably wherever they could find a perch. At the top of the lorry was a mound covered by flowers. Only a small exposed head revealed that this was the corpse of the Mahatma, the first dead body I had ever seen. As it passed in front of us mourners broke ranks in that silent crowd to step forward and throw flowers in its path, raising their voices to bless Gandhi. '*Amar rahe* – stay immortal.'

In a few hours there would be nothing left of the Mahatma but ashes, and on the radio the Indian Prime Minister would announce to the nation, 'The light has gone out of our lives.'

When I grew older I learned the names of some of the old people riding on the lorry, and realized I had watched a human pageant of those who had fought for India's freedom taking the symbol of that freedom movement to his funeral pyre.

Then, I had only seen a mound covered in marigold garlands. It was not a frightening sight, and it certainly wasn't glamorous. Even as very small children we could feel the heavy-heartedness, the dignity of the occasion – somehow more real because it was so shabby. Just a lorry, a corpse circled by people weeping silently, watched by grieving Indians who knew that independent India, only six months old, had already lost her innocence.

Years later I saw Richard Attenborough's film *Gandhi*. In the film Gandhi's funeral cortège was a huge military affair with gun carriages and rows of serried soldiers marching with slow and solemn precision to the beat of funereal drums. Wondering if my own memories could have been so warped by time, I asked one of the Mahatma's grandsons about the vast gap between my recollection and what I had seen on celluloid.

'Briefly that ceremony did take place,' he admitted. 'Even though Gandhi-ji never wanted a production made of his death. It was invented by Nehru and Mountbatten. For the record.'

What record, I wondered. Soldiers? Gun carriages? For the disciple of non-violence? All those uniforms and all that gold braid for the man who dared to wear a loincloth to his meeting with the King Emperor of India?

If ever anything would have been abhorrent to Gandhi, smacking of the very colonialism he had done everything in his power to end, it would have been the idea of a state funeral.

Yet in one of the most imperious *grands gestes* of the twentieth century, Gandhi had insisted that Lord Louis Mountbatten, the last British Viceroy of India, be invited by Indians to become our first head of state. It was an eccentric demand, but consistent. Indeed, for years Gandhi had seen no reason to expel the British from India.

'If they can govern justly,' he had argued in the middle of a freedom movement, 'what difference does it make?'

He only changed his mind after the limited self-government Britain had promised India did not materialize, and the Empire refused to lift the tax on salt in a continent where Indians needed salt to live.

Stating that he now believed Britain incapable of just government, Gandhi wrote to the British Viceroy, 'On bended knee I asked for bread and you gave me stone instead.'

Then he embarked on his famous Salt March to the sea to make illegal salt – the non-violent movement of civil disobedience that would dislodge the British Raj.

By inviting Mountbatten to become free India's first head of state Gandhi wanted to dispel India's hatred of her past colonial masters. He was indifferent to Mountbatten's race. Gandhi never doubted the equality of all human beings. He wanted justice. That's why he could wear a loincloth to Buckingham Palace. But his death became an opportunity for Mountbatten and Nehru to show the world how well they could do state occasions.

I guess I was lucky. Even if he was dead, even if I was hardly more than a baby, I saw the actual Mahatma. Not a Mahatma invented for history or politics or films.

Alas, poor Gandhi.

Who had pleaded that the Indian National Congress was a freedom movement, not a political party, and should be disbanded when India became free.

Who had showed us that non-violence and a proud humility went hand in hand.

Who had believed that Indians would govern themselves with greater justice than their colonial masters.

He did not even reach his funeral pyre before his luck ran out.

Sixteen

Finding the Centre

When I attended Bombay University the college at which I was a resident student was run by nuns – satisfying two requirements for my mother's peace of mind. The necessity for higher education. The necessity for stern chaperonage.

Although now a convent, by bizarre circumstance the college had originally housed the harem of the Maharajah of Indore, and the Maharajah's frowning visage still crowned the pink stucco pillars, watching disapprovingly as we convent girls carried on the way convent girls do, even though the nuns did their best to control our high spirits.

So naturally when I saw the sign up on the college bulletin board prohibiting all students from going to a particular area in the city because of a huge demonstration expected that afternoon, I immediately caught the next bus to the forbidden. It was my first opportunity to participate in a serious political event.

The demonstration was a key moment in India's democratic development. Kerala, the southernmost state in India – with the highest literacy rate in the country – had, in a free and fair election, elected a communist government. Inexplicably, Prime Minister Nehru had overruled the election, although the right of every state in the republic to choose its own state government was enshrined in our constitution. In fact, the Indian states had considerable autonomy from the central government in Delhi except in times of 'emergency', and there had been no emergency.

The thought of India's constitution being betrayed by Nehru was inconceivable to us. He had spent years in British jails demanding democracy. When we achieved democracy, Nehru had led the National Congress party to victory in three successive elections. All our conscious lives, he was the only Prime Minister we had ever known. He had encouraged us to call him Uncle Nehru, had improved the homespun look of Mahatma Gandhi with a perennial rosebud in his coat, and kept tiger cubs in the gardens of the beautiful Prime Ministerial residence.

True, he had recently shown an Achilles heel by supporting the appointment of his daughter, Indira Gandhi, as president of the party organization. But none of us thought of this as the beginning of a terrible nepotism that would, fifteen years later, lead to the shut-down of democracy in the whole of India.

We had not acquainted ourselves sufficiently with Indian history to know that Nehru had been himself anointed leader of the Indian National Congress by his own father while travelling to a nationalist convention in 1929. The young Nehru had apparently blushed at the obscene suggestion, but his father had argued that there was no need for such formalities as an election, and by the time the overnight train reached Lahore Nehru had stopped resisting.

Because we did not know these things we did not consider it particularly sinister that now Nehru, as his father
had done before him, had placed this political party – so
great that it was said the two largest organizations in the
world were the Catholic Church and the Indian National
Congress – in the hands of his only child, Indira, who had
prevailed upon him to dismiss the Kerala government.

This afternoon in 1959 the huge gathering in the Oval
gardens of Bombay was to demonstrate against the first
major act of corruption in free India's public life. Though
I was on my way to the demonstration for adolescent and
sensationalist reasons, even I thought what Nehru and his
daughter had done was pretty rum. And when I joined
that sea of demonstrators, two hundred thousand strong,
I experienced a satisfying sense of one-ness. Perhaps it had
all been some terrible mistake and this aberration would
soon be put to rights.

It was a humid day, and the overcast sky seemed to
press down on the immense crowd packed into the park.
Squeezing past people perspiring heavily in the heavy air
I made my way towards the front of the demonstration.
There were thousands of trade-unionists holding placards
claiming that communism was a legitimate road to social
justice. There were newspapermen. There were ordinary
citizens who objected to an action that smacked of the
imperial fiats of the British Raj. There were people from
Kerala, shocked by the attack on their democratic rights,
accusing Nehru of dismissing their government because it
had recently enacted laws giving land to the landless.

Such was the scale of the demonstration that every
policeman in Bombay had been called out in case things
got out of control. In the middle of that huge demonstration I was suddenly surrounded by a cordon of

demonstrators who urged me to leave. I objected strongly. I wanted to be part of the action. The trade-unionists around me were courteous but firm. This was not a game, they pointed out. The police had tear gas and were preparing to use it. There would be confusion, demonstrators would fall and perhaps be trampled when the tear-gas canisters were fired into that tightly packed crowd. No one wanted to be responsible for harm coming to a lady.

Under the circumstances I had little option but to agree to be escorted from the park by eight men, linking arms to make way for me through the crowd. A few minutes later the firing began.

In the years that followed, there would be other demonstrations when state governments were dismissed, but the police would no longer hold their fire until the women and children had left.

And we would learn through bitter experience how the strain of centralizing power could make the republic creak like an overloaded ship, its cargo of disparities too heavy a weight to keep it afloat.

Seventeen

Congress Culture

After studying at Cambridge University I returned to Bombay, and during an academic gathering I met a poet, who invited me to visit him for tea. The poet was very exact about the directions to his home, since his poverty condemned him to live in the huge slum on the way to Bombay airport inhabited some said by fifty thousand people, some said by a hundred thousand people.

The poet had been born a Hindu belonging to the lowest caste until he had converted to the Buddhist faith, as Dr Ambedkar had done ten years earlier, watched by half a million untouchables. Now the poet was a Dalit. The word meant downtrodden. More than that, he was now a Dalit Panther.

His creed was Dr Ambedkar's famous speech to untouchables who had failed after five years of non-violent demonstration to gain entrance to a Hindu temple.

'If you want self-respect,' Dr Ambedkar had said, 'change your religion.

'If you want equality change your religion.

'If you want power change your religion.

'That religion which forbids humanitarian beh
between men is not a religion but a penalty.

'That religion which regards the recognition of h
dignity as a sin is not a religion but a sickness.

'That religion which allows one to touch a foul animal
but not a man is not a religion but a madness.'

In Bombay the powerful speech had been adopted by
educated untouchables, who had formed themselves into
a militant movement after converting to the Buddhist faith.
They called themselves the Dalit Panthers.

I was familiar with the term 'panther'. During the years
I had spent in England, the Vietnam War was at its height,
demonstrations were a daily affair and the main body of
student opinion had been sympathetic to the cause of the
Black Panthers, the black militants in America.

Back in India I discovered Indian university students
were also reading the jailed Eldridge Cleaver's book *Soul
on Ice*, and women regularly paraded the streets in front of
the American Embassy in Delhi with placards demanding
FREE ANGELA DAVIS.

And now, in 1969, I found myself having tea with a
Dalit Panther in a shack constructed from tin sheets, bits
of wood, discarded posters, torn sarongs – any protection
from the monsoon rain pouring down with such force that
it had flooded the camp's mud alleys, turning them into
running streams in which pieces of construction material
were floating disconsolately.

While the poet squatted on the floor and heated water
in a pan over a kerosene burner to make tea, I sat on a
plank of wood raised on bricks surreptitiously examining
his home. Everything was in its place. A few garments
hung on a rope that extended across the shelter, tied from

one pole to another. Above the kerosene burner he had nailed a picture of Dr Ambedkar into the tin wall.

He unlocked a small trunk, removing a packet of tea and two steel tumblers. I peered over his shoulder into the trunk. Books and papers were neatly stacked to one side; cooking utensils and paper packets filled with rice, flour, lentils stacked on the other side.

'They say the British used Divide and Rule to control India but the Congress Party has perfected it,' the poet said angrily as he brewed the tea. 'As for the Congress culture . . .' His rage would not allow him to complete the sentence.

He didn't have to. I knew what he meant. After twenty years of unchallenged power the great Indian National Congress had grown moribund, its leaders arguing over the spoils of office, its party committee warning its members, 'Congress personnel is hopelessly divided – factionalism is pervasive – dissensions and mutual vilification create a revulsion of feelings against the Congress among the people.'

The poet handed me a glass of tea and spoke of his hatred of what he called the 'Congress Culture' practised by politicians who cynically retained power by playing on the fears of the country's minorities – the Muslims, the lower castes, the Buddhists, the Christians.

'Are you thinking of entering politics?' I enquired.

'A poor man like me?' he asked incredulously. 'Against the money and muscle of these politicians who rule over us like kings?'

He went to the kerosene stove to heat some more water and I surreptitiously hitched up my sari to avoid the water running in rivulets across the mud floor.

Turning, the poet saw me.

He waved his arms helplessly to indicate the squalor of the camp, the water running across the floor, the sodden cloth covering the entrance to his shack.

Pointing at the picture on his wall he told me bitterly that he had the national flag tattooed on his buttocks, because the constitution was only good for wiping the national arse.

'Dr Ambedkar was wrong. Changing a religion means nothing. Elections mean nothing. For people like us power can only come from the barrel of a gun.'

Eighteen

Non-Violence

In 1978 an Indian magazine asked me to go to the north-east border state of Assam, home to twenty million people, and write about the largest non-violent movement India had seen since Mahatma Gandhi had used non-violence to end the British Raj.

Non-violence may have expelled the British from India but our first lesson in freedom was the violence of Partition, and in Assam I discovered that we have not learned our lesson well.

Its rice fields stretching to Bangladesh on one side, its wooded hills rising to China's borders on the other, Assam is connected to India only by a narrow corridor of land. But the attempt to capture India's attention had mobilized hundreds of thousands of Assamese into a non-violent movement that had already closed schools, factories, shops and India's major oil refinery for nearly a year.

It was dusk when I reached the capital of Assam and drove to the hill temple that is Assam's holiest place of pilgrimage.

Standing on the hillside high above the mighty Brahmaputra River, I tried to understand this movement whose ranks swelled daily with newcomers prepared to defend what tourist brochures called 'The Land of the Red River and the Blue Hills'.

In the temple courtyard a frangipani tree was dropping white blossoms on the black stones, the slender petals spinning like hexagons against the darkening sky. Below the temple, the setting sun was throwing the islands in the vast sweep of water into red relief. River steamers from the days of the British Empire, still bearing their battered old Jardine Henderson signs, crossed the crimson water of the great river as mist closed over the fishing villages on the distant bank. Inside the temple the priest had begun the evening devotions, chanting a melancholy melody that seemed to evoke Assam's separation from the rest of India.

We had done little to dispel that sense of isolation. In 1962, when the Chinese Army had invaded India through Assam, Prime Minister Nehru had withdrawn our ill-equipped troops from the occupied state with his infamous radio address, 'My heart bleeds for the people of Assam.'

Then in 1971 the war for the new nation of Bangladesh had pushed waves of war-weary refugees over India's borders into Assam. They were still there, and the Assamese were demonstrating against what they considered a new occupation. Now Prime Minister Indira Gandhi had declared the movement the work of foreign agitators and sent in the Indian Army to disband the protestors and open the oil refinery.

So I could sympathize with the angry young engineer who had asked me, 'We are fighting another invasion and Nehru's daughter sends the Army to fire on us! Is she mad? Is it our fault that the millions of foreigners who are over-running us today don't speak Chinese?'

But as I watched the lanterns swaying on the steamers far below me and the river turning black in the fading light, I could not help wondering how long Assam's movement to expel foreigners would limit itself to foreigners. How long before it turned on other Indians?

The next day as my car approached the oil installation, I could see large painted hoardings warning *No Entry. Restricted Area. No Unauthorized Personnel*. Obeying the ominous signs at the entrance gates, we stopped. A guard came out of the guardhouse with a large security ledger. My driver carefully filled in the required information. *Time. Number of Visitors*. Under the heading *Purpose of Visit* he carefully wrote down *Picketing*. I borrowed the ledger, flipping through its pages. On each page the *Purpose of Visit* column repeated its pedantic entry: *Picketing. Picketing. Picketing*.

Despite the ledger entries, I was unprepared for the enormity of the crowds inside the sprawling oil installations. There were people everywhere – on the verandahs, on the grass, on any piece of ground where there was some shade from the fierce sun. Banners proclaimed the cause: *We Will Give Our Blood But Not Our Oil*. Under a portrait of Mahatma Gandhi was emblazoned *Uphold My Teachings. Uphold the Constitution. Kill Me Not Again by Killing the Peaceful Picketers*.

Thousands of boys were lying in rows on the ground, dressed in sarongs for comfort, equipped with cigarettes, radios and magazines for another night of civil disobedience. Facing them was a long double-storeyed building crowded with women preparing food. A man with a megaphone was shouting out instructions to the newcomers: where to go for water, where to sleep, where the toilets were.

Buses disgorged increasing numbers of picketers next to a wall where a line of giggling schoolgirls sat, dangling their feet over a gutter and comparing ear-rings.

I asked them if they had met with any resistance from their parents when they joined the picket lines.

'Of course. Our parents told us there are too many boys here. Spending the nights like this, our reputations will be destroyed. Afterwards, who will marry us?'

The giggling got louder until I enquired how they felt about the Army being called out to disband the pickets and start the oil pumping again.

'I would be proud to die for the cause,' said one girl with absolute conviction. 'We have taken the vow of supreme sacrifice.'

'We are not afraid of the Army,' declared another girl, whose father was a priest at the temple. 'How can the Army be violent to us when we ourselves are non-violent?'

Because India's need for oil is so great, I thought.

Still, a picket official graciously accepted my congratulations on the wonderful organization.

'Though we didn't really organize anything,' he told me proudly. 'It just happened. Was it Oscar Wilde who said, "Crisis needs no rehearsal"?' Our movement is a spontaneous mass response to a crisis.'

'Chaos needs no rehearsal either,' I reminded him.

'Why chaos? What can the Army do against such numbers?' He leaned towards me confidentially. 'You know, at our first meetings we asked people to give up going to the cinema and smoking cigarettes until there was not a foreigner left on our soil. They didn't agree. Then we asked if they would give up their lives. Everyone shouted yes.'

I immediately lit a cigarette. Who was I to

the hundreds and thousands of people who agreed that it was easier to give up your life than to give up smoking?

And perhaps both living and smoking are easier to give up than anger. The anger of the non-Assamese university lecturer who demanded, 'Peaceful? This movement? Ask my wife!'

The wife, serving tea, said, 'I have lived all over India but I never knew I was a Bengali, not an Indian, until I came here. I am watching what is happening and wondering where it will stop. Women I have cuddled in my lap when they were themselves children now let their own children stand outside my gate yelling, "Bengali dogs! Get out!" '

Her husband added wearily, 'I tell my students, once you think you belong only to a particular part of the country you deprive yourselves of the wealth of the whole country. Unfortunately, the real fuel of this movement is emotionalism. And in these circumstances anything can happen.'

Two nights later I gained some idea of what could happen. The vast and generally peaceful movement was nonetheless full of the simple passion and simplistic rhetoric that breeds intimidation.

A storm was threatening as I reached a village already a casualty of that rhetoric. Inside the crowded mud hut insects buzzed around a single hurricane lantern and small children, their eyes huge in the lamplight, listened in fearful fascination to their elders. Outside, waves of fireflies made a confusion of the dark as the voices around me intoned a checklist of horror.

'They beat seventeen men to death in the next village because their ancestors came from another part of India.'

'We were lucky. We repulsed the first wave of killers

with bamboo sticks. Then other wounded villagers came running to us for help. Together, we were enough to frighten the killers away.'

'Twenty-eight villages were put to the torch last night. Why?'

Why indeed? Whatever happened to India's proud pluralism? Whatever happened to non-violence?

Nineteen

Good Housekeeping

Non-violence was India's creed, but by the time I reached Assam India had fought three wars in ten years, and I had witnessed the last.

In 1971, under Indira Gandhi, we had fought a war with Pakistan that had enabled a mutinous East Pakistan to become the independent nation of Bangladesh. I was reporting that war for television, so I was present when the Indian soldiers were greeted by a delirious Bangladeshi population. I saw the brilliant splashes of colour as gladioli and canna lilies were pressed into metallic gun barrels instead of bayonets.

In the company of the Indian Jewish general who had written the terms of the cease-fire I watched a Sikh general take the surrender of the enemy Army, and with profound relief I saw our young soldiers were obeying their Christian commanding officer by showing only respect to the Bangladeshi girls who had been kept by the hated occupying troops as comfort women in their trenches.

Soon the Indian Army would again distinguish itself by

safeguarding the honour of women – but this time the women would be Indian.

The year was 1975 and the prevailing situation was called a revolution. In fact it was a rather domestic affair concerning an election in Gujarat – a state of hard-working farmers and entrepreneurs who were finding the cost of living too high and whose wives had taken to demonstrating.

The movement against prices in Gujarat started peacefully enough. As the birthplace of Mahatma Gandhi, non-violent expression was second nature to Gujarat, and the revolution consisted largely of housewives in the state capital pouring out of their doorways at sunset, the hour when they should have been lighting lamps in front of family altars prior to preparing the family's evening meal.

Finding it impossible to make ends meet and feed their families, the housewives waited until the street lamps came on. Then they beat their metal platters, their *thalis*, with wooden rolling-pins to express their dissatisfaction with rising prices.

The practice rapidly spread throughout the state and within days the national press was calling the ire of the housewives the Thali Revolution. Needing no signal but the setting sun, no provocation but rocketing prices, in every part of the state, from its small towns and villages to its diamond centres and ports, the women of Gujarat banged away at their *thalis* – creating such a din that the state echoed with their displeasure.

Still, the noise was not so great that it could be heard a thousand miles away in Delhi, but a solid month of this behaviour was making Prime Minister Indira Gandhi nervous. And another factor was involved – a politician's nightmare.

A man called Raj Narain was accusing the Prime Minister of rigging her personal election to Parliament. He had contested her seat and claimed Mrs Gandhi had misused government funds and officials to defeat him. In fact he had wrapped a green bandana on his head and grown a beard, vowing he would not shave until the Indian courts reversed the Prime Minister's parliamentary election.

At first he had been dismissed as a clown annoying the Prime Minister who enjoyed the admiration of the nation. Then the Prime Minister's own actions became erratic. She permitted her inexperienced younger son, Sanjay, to acquire a government licence to make 50,000 'people's' cars a year for his Maruti company, a licence repeatedly denied to other Indian companies familiar with the manufacture of automobiles. Four hundred acres of land were requisitioned on the outskirts of the capital for the factory premises, evicting the inhabitants of three entire villages. Government financial institutions were pressured into giving Maruti unsecured loans as each attempt to produce a car resulted in embarrassing failures. Finally the Reserve Bank of India, the country's central financial institution, intervened, informing state banks that further unsecured loans would undermine the basis of the country's credit policies. Meanwhile, another company owned by Sanjay Gandhi, his elder brother Rajiv and their respective wives was discovered to be acting as an agent for government contracts.

In Parliament, critics across the political spectrum were demanding a judicial enquiry into what they variously called 'a disgrace to democracy', 'corruption and nepotism', 'unlimited corruption'. When the Prime Minister blocked every attempt at an enquiry, in 1973 the entire

Parliamentary Opposition walked out of the House to express their displeasure.

So by 1975 Indians were beginning to pay greater attention to the accusations made by the man in the green bandana – especially the housewives beating away at their *thalis* in the state of Gujarat, where an election was to be held.

Rattled by the man in the bandana's insistence that Indira Gandhi had won her own parliamentary election dishonestly, the people of Gujarat were determined not to be robbed of the legitimate results of their state election.

Stay up all night, they exhorted each other as the date for polling approached. Guard the ballot boxes. Throw cordons of women and children around the polling booths so that no one can exchange votes under cover of darkness. Oversee the counting.

All this proved too much for the Prime Minister. Describing the Thali Revolution as a CIA plot, and then, with her unique gift for paranoia, as a plot by Amnesty International, she sent in the Indian Army to subdue the housewives of Gujarat.

If the housewives of Gujarat had, as their tribal brethren had done two decades earlier, solemnly exposed their backsides to the symbol of Delhi's imperialism, who knows what the outcome might have been? Instead, they continued to come out at dusk and beat their *thalis* with their rolling-pins, deafening the embarrassed troops.

These are not housewives, insisted the agitated Prime Minister from Delhi. They are *agents provocateurs*. Use tear gas, rubber bullets, yes, live rounds, until this threat to the nation's security is terminated.

At her command the officers of the Indian Army ordered their troops to do something that had only happened once before, when nationalists were making illegal salt in defiance of British laws. Then, a British commanding officer had ordered the Royal Garhwal Rifles to fire on the peaceful protestors. The Garwhal Rifles had refused to follow orders.

Now, receiving the Prime Minister of India's directive, once again Indian troops reversed their arms, informing Delhi that the Indian Army did not shoot at Indian citizens.

Twenty

Hereditary Democracy

For the first twenty-five years of modern India's history our elected representatives generally conducted themselves as servants of the people, concerned for the nation's welfare.

But a crack had already appeared in India's shiny new democracy. Nehru dismissed an elected state assembly, setting a precedent which his successors would exploit whenever they felt threatened.

As for our claim to non-violence, under the proud Nehru we fought a war with China, under the meek Shashtri we fought a war with Pakistan. Then Mrs Gandhi prosecuted a second war with Pakistan, which helped to create the nation of Bangladesh.

Having split the National Congress and taken its largest faction to a landslide victory with the slogan Remove Poverty, at the height of her popularity Mrs Gandhi turned dynastic, fearful of any political challenge.

Ignoring democratic norms, she dismissed state governments at will and elevated unelected family members to positions of power. To ratify her increasingly bizarre behaviour, she manipulated undistinguished but obedient politicians into the highest office in the land.

'If she had asked me to clean her latrine I would have done so,' observed one Head of State naïvely. 'But she asked me to be President of India.'

India was changing from a democracy into a court. Soon it would become a police state.

For the next twenty years horrified Indians would watch in disbelief as our politicians forged ever more unholy alliances to keep themselves in power, and succeeded only in losing their own lives in bloodbaths of their own creation.

Created from a dream of non-violence, India would become a land of armed crack-downs and assassins, of bullet-proof screens and police cordons and bombs.

Presiding over an exponential growth of corruption in public life, our leaders would depend on criminals to ensure electoral success, and soon the criminals would themselves enter Parliament.

The rich diversity on which our survival depended would be used against us – caste against caste, religious group against religious group – until hatred became the pattern of our democracy.

And the Indian Army – the third-largest standing army in the world, a volunteer force so proud of its campaign histories – would be ruthlessly used by India's leaders to force trials of strength with the Indian people, making tragedy inevitable.

Twenty-One

Mass Transit

One summer night in 1975, while the nation slept, the Prime Minister ended democracy in India.

Indira Gandhi declared a State of Emergency 'to defend India's unity and integrity'.

For goodness' sake! What on earth had threatened Indian integrity? Well, on June 12 the courts had found Indira Gandhi guilty of 'using government personnel to further her electoral prospects'. She was forbidden from holding any elected office for the next six years. In view of her lofty office, she was given twenty days to appeal to the Supreme Court of India, but she could no longer act as Prime Minister of India.

'A week is a long time in politics,' the British Prime Minister Harold Wilson once said. But twenty whole days? For a leader who could already sense the sharks circling?

The clock was ticking, so on June 16, at three o'clock in the morning, the Delhi police handcuffed Mrs Gandhi's political opponents and carted them off to jail. That same night power was cut off to newspaper printing presses. When the power was turned on again, the censored newspapers printed blank pages with black borders, announcing the death of India's freedom in their obituary columns.

A week later the President of India declared that an imperilled India was now under the Maintenance of Internal Security Act. Indian citizens could no longer question the grounds on which they were detained. Or invoke habeas corpus – the court's right to view a prisoner and establish that he was well, or even alive.

The proclamation was followed by midnight raids and mass arrests across the nation – political opponents, dissenting members of the Prime Minister's own party, students, social workers, journalists, teachers, judges, union leaders, and thousands of innocent bystanders. Even a group of astonished hippies.

The writings of Mahatma Gandhi, Nehru and other Indian patriots on the right to freedom were proscribed, Mahatma Gandhi's own newspaper closed by government fiat.

And with half the nation's elected representatives in jail, the Constitution of India was amended four times. The first amendment prevented any legal challenge to the declaration of the Emergency. The second nullified retroactively the judgment of the court against Mrs Gandhi for corrupt practices, and deprived the courts of jurisdiction over any future electoral malpractices by a Prime Minister.

The third amendment gave India's Prime Minister permanent immunity from any civil or criminal proceedings – not only while occupying office but before assuming office, and just to be on the safe side, after leaving office.

The fourth amendment was particularly poignant.

Having lost their fundamental rights, Indian citizens were now given a list of fundamental duties.

Neutered of its constitutional power, the Supreme Court over-ruled Mrs Gandhi's sentence. Only Justice Khanna, next in line to become the Chief Justice of India, argued that all these constitutional amendments had become meaningless, since depriving a person of life and liberty without the authority of law was to remove the distinction between a lawless society and one governed by law.

As if to prove his argument, the offices of over two hundred rebellious Delhi lawyers were bulldozed to the ground. The lawyers marched, black-robed, in silent protest on the Supreme Court. They were promptly arrested as arsonists and looters.

But the poor who objected when their homes were bulldozed for beautification of the city were given no reason for their arrests. And they had no redress against a new population control programme in which government employees were given sterilization quotas which had to be filled if the employees wanted promotion, or even to keep their jobs.

Villagers were rounded up, police cornered the city's poor, people died of botched operations, doctors who objected to the lack of hygiene were jailed. Meanwhile, nationalized television and radio kept up a barrage of propaganda telling the nation we had never had it so good. After all, each sterilized person was being given a transistor radio by the government.

With awesome inevitability, Mrs Gandhi raised her younger son, Sanjay Gandhi, to become an unelected centre of absolute power, second only to herself in the country.

Equally inevitably, having ruthlessly silenced all dissension, the Prime Minister and her son believed the massive organized crowds were spontaneous displays of a nation's adulation. And across the border Pakistan was going to the polls.

Determined to prove to the world that she was indisputably the voice of India, assured by intelligence reports that victory was a certainty, Mrs Gandhi suddenly called a snap election to legitimize her actions.

The elections were to take place in a mere six weeks, but most of India's political leaders were still in jail. To prove the election was not a fiction they were now released – on parole, required to report their movements to their local police, forbidden to travel.

There was every expectation that Mrs Gandhi would win. The state-owned radio and television companies were pumping out government propaganda. Newspapers were censored. Now the Government raised the salaries of millions of government employees – teachers, factory workers, army personnel, bureaucrats – certain that self-interest would guarantee electoral success.

Everyone knew – though they could not speak of it for fear of being overheard and reported to the police – that India's future rode on this election. What Mahatma Gandhi had done in the 1930s with his Salt March had to be done again in the 1970s, a silent protest of gargantuan proportions. And six weeks was all the time the nation had.

I attended a series of rallies in Delhi in those weeks, learned about through word of mouth. At each rally the crowds grew larger, proving the bush telegraph to be as effective a means of communication as electronics when there is something urgent to convey. While Indira Gandhi addressed meetings in the main parks, with all the attendant panoply of state – police cordons, massive platforms, free transport to bring reluctant audiences back and forth – we strained to hear paroled leaders standing on soap-boxes with only a megaphone for amplification.

On the road leading into Delhi University I listened to the redoubtable Madame Pandit, with her Chinese collars and blue-rinsed hair, urging us to vote for freedom. Although she was Nehru's sister, she had needed no nepotistic appointments. She had been the first woman president of the General Assembly of the United Nations, and had played a distinguished role in the struggle for India's freedom. Now, despite the fact that she was already in her eighties, Madame Pandit had come out of political retirement to hold meetings all over the capital, appalled by the smashing of the Indian democratic process by her own niece.

At one rally Madame Pandit was speaking to us in Hindustani when she noticed the arrival of camera crews. She broke off her speech to enquire who they were. Learning they were European reporters she proceeded with her impassioned speech but translated her words into English, German and French for the television cameras. It was a *tour de force* performance. Such effortless sophistication – it made you proud to be an Indian.

Then, only days before the momentous general election, a meeting was held at night in the walled city of Old Delhi, inside the great Friday Mosque built by the Moghul emperors to face the Red Fort that was the seat of their Empire. For five hundred years this particular area of Delhi had been the goal of those who wished to gain power over India. It was here that the victorious British soldiers had built their army barracks on the harem of the last Moghul emperor, here that the Union Jack was lowered and the Indian flag unfurled when India became a free nation.

The sun had long since set by the time I reached the rally but crowds were still streaming into the grounds of the mosque. To discourage attendance electricity to the entire area had been cut off by the city administration, and for once the brooding vastness of the mosque dwarfed the narrow streets of the old city crowded with veiled women. Many of its residents were Muslim families who still lived in the same sixteenth-century houses, with the interior courtyards and latticed stone balconies and narrow stairways, that their ancestors had occupied. For two long years they had endured the excesses of the Emergency – seen respected elders, or young boys not yet pubescent, forcibly sterilized to fulfil government quotas; seen shops crushed into rubble under the bulldozers' inexorable advance.

Now the darkness, lit only by kerosene lanterns and huge torches, added a sombreness to the occasion, almost a magnificence, allowing us to see the great mosque as it must have been seen by the Moghuls themselves, its massive lines looming above us undiminished by the neon strips which would ordinarily have illuminated the bazaars and warrens of streets of the old city. Two- and three-storey houses ringed the mosque. Women in billowing burnouses crowded at the dimly lit balconies like the silhouetted audience in some theatre, their shapes negated by folds of black cloth.

There was no room for us on the wide sandstone steps leading up to the platform, where lanterns threw the features of the speakers into grotesque relief as they addressed the crowds spilling down the steps and into the streets. We could hardly hear the speakers but we knew from their shapes who they were. The Imam of the mosque, spokesman of Muslim sentiment, shared the steps with the leader of the right-wing Hindus. Sworn enemies from the time of Partition, theirs was a blood hatred. Yet together they were exhorting us to exert our democratic rights. There was the greatest snob in India, Madame Pandit, her hair purple in the lamplight, unable to find a place on those crowded stairs, sitting at the feet of the leader of the untouchables. Ignoring the separations of caste, of class, of gods, the speakers shared the crowded platform while we stood there straining to hear them remind us how our ballots could change history.

Suddenly the women weren't up on the balconies any more. They were among us, their faces exposed, cloth panels thrown resolutely above their heads, breaking the enormity of purdah to rally against the leader whom they held responsible for dishonouring their menfolk, destroying their homes.

A fortnight later the counting had ended and the Government was preparing its victory celebrations.

At two o'clock in the morning I waited with thousands of other Indians in front of the offices of the *Indian Express* newspaper. We were milling in the street at that ungodly hour because the newspaper's correspondents were telephoning through the election results from all over the nation, results which the shocked government television and radio stations were not announcing.

Every few minutes a journalist came out of the offices, handed a piece of paper to a thin clerk in grey trousers scribbling with chalk onto a blackboard, raced back inside again. While we held our breaths the clerk scribbled the latest election results onto the spotlighted blackboard. Each time a candidate of Mrs Gandhi's party lost a seat, money was flung at him for bringing good news and he blinked at us in surprise through the currency floating like confetti over his head.

When Mrs Gandhi lost her own parliamentary seat by a massive margin, women began flinging their jewellery at the clerk.

In all the cheering I heard someone say, 'She got what she deserved. Why did she trouble the poor?'

Twenty-Two

Losing It

The Emergency was India's watershed, compromising the President and the Supreme Court who rubber-stamped it; the bureaucrats and police who enforced it; the national radio and television who lauded it, unchallenged by a gagged press.

Determined that Indians should understand the process by which their liberty could so easily be robbed, India's new Prime Minister Morarji Desai held a public enquiry into the causes of the Emergency and the hearings were broadcast on national television. While Parliament reversed Mrs Gandhi's constitutional amendments, day after day hundreds of people appeared before the Shah Commission to describe their experiences – which too often included torture. Their evidence was then published in the Shah Commission Report, providing a unique examination of India's democracy.

One thing the hearings proved conclusively. We desperately needed political alternatives to control the excesses of the party that had ruled India these thirty years. But our first alternative, the Janata Party, was formed under the most unpropititious circumstances – its leaders on parole, unable to meet and resolve their conflicting agendas. In power those leaders were soon imitating the behaviour of their Congress predecessors.

As the Janata Party disintegrated, Indira Gandhi toured the nation, denying responsibility for the excesses of the Emergency and offering a Government that Works. At the next election, having no political alternative, the nation voted Mrs Gandhi back to power. Copies of the Shah Commission's report on the Emergency were immediately seized and destroyed.

Now the scramble for power was on in earnest. While we spent the next decades looking for that elusive prize of a genuinely multi-party system our leaders looked for more ways to divide us.

But at least we knew that the categorical verdict against the Emergency had safeguarded our democracy forever.

Alas, we had not thought to defend ourselves against the politics of religion.

We were so certain no Indian politician would dare use religion to gain power. Not after the horrors of Partition. Everyone knew religion was India's line of no return. Beyond that line lay chaos.

A social reformer called 'the conscience of the nation' knew India better than us. Minutes after the Emergency was declared, the terminally ill Jayaprakash Narayan was pulled from his bed and taken off to jail, the first casualty of India's lost liberty. Turning to his jailers he explained Mrs Gandhi's behaviour by reciting the famous Sanskrit lines that describe the madness of Sita, the god Rama's wife.

In Indian mythology Sita and her brother-in-law Laxman are wandering the jungle, waiting for Rama to find them. Before Laxman goes to hunt for food, he draws three lines in the dust, warning Sita that if she steps over them he can no longer protect her. But Sita sees a golden deer through the trees, calling in Rama's voice, and she steps over the lines of protection into chaos.

That night when embarrassed jailers put handcuffs on a leader who had walked at Mahatma Gandhi's side during the movement for India's freedom, Jayaprakash Narayan recited,

> *No one sees a golden deer*
> *No one hears a golden deer*
> *Until the times are bad and the mind is disordered.*

Now the times were again bad.

We were being told that our rich pluralism, the diversity that defined us, was a sickness, an alien concept of Western secularism grafted onto India.

We were about to face our second watershed.

India's leaders had seen the golden deer of power running through India's trees and it was calling to them in God's voice.

Twenty-Three

God's Work

When Britain's expatriate Sikhs celebrated the three hundredth anniversary of their faith in the Royal Albert Hall in London, they invited the Indian writer Khushwant Singh to speak on the occasion. Singh had once been a member of the Indian diplomatic mission in London. His novel *Train to Pakistan* was considered a classic on the horrors of Partition. And he was a Sikh.

Unfazed by the red velvet chairs and royal boxes of the Albert Hall, Singh rose to his feet and shouted lustily to the packed chamber, 'Beloved ones, do you remember the taste of unleavened bread?'

There was a roar of response from the turbanned audience, hearing the earthy language of the Punjab farmers. Back in India, their industrious relatives were turning the Punjab into the granary of India – those relatives who were not in the Indian Armed Forces, mostly as front-line troops.

'And do you remember the taste of black lentils?' Whistles and stamping shook the chamber – nostalgia for the diet to which the audience ascribed their robust strength.

'And what about the taste of mustard spinach and sugar-cane juice?'

Cheering Sikhs were on their feet, shouting their battlecry, 'Victory to the guru's faithful! Victory to his men of truth!'

It was a common response to anything that moved them. The Sikhs are a people proud of their martial history, which is why they still wear their long hair under a turban in the symbol by which Sikhs once identified each other on the battlefield defending their religion. In fact, during the religious persecution of the fanatical Moghul Emperor Aurangzeb, even Hindu families often gave one son to the Sikh faith, to keep their line alive.

Yet in their holiest shrine, the Golden Temple of Amritsar, symbolic of the spiritual power of God, with its library containing books collected over five centuries and manuscripts written by the gurus of their faith, serenity is sacrosanct.

It was, that is, until Mrs Gandhi and her younger son supported an obscure Sikh priest named Bhindranwale to bring down the elected state government of Punjab.

Armed with automatic rifles, confident of the central government's protection, the priest and his followers entered the Golden Temple. From the safety of the temple the priest declared anyone not a Sikh should be evicted from the state. While he issued fanatical edicts his followers beat up Sikhs who raised their voices in protest, shot dead the Sikh Inspector General of Police and intimidated non-Sikhs into fleeing. Soon Punjab was an armed camp. Inside the state Hindus were being terrorised; outside the state Sikhs were being terrorised. For the first time in India's history, there was hatred between Hindu and Sikh.

On the grounds of restoring stability, Mrs Gandhi assumed control of the Punjab. But the monster she had created so unthinkingly could no longer be controlled. The priest was now so powerful he was being courted by other political parties. He was now so powerful he didn't want to be courted – he wanted his own country. Having run out of options, she dispatched the Indian Army to oust the priest, and in the pitched battle the great library of the Sikhs was destroyed, innocent worshippers killed by crossfire.

Blood had at last stained the white marble floor of the Golden Temple.

To avenge those deaths Mrs Gandhi was herself shot by a Sikh bodyguard even as she was campaigning for a new general election. Squads of thugs responded by murdering thousands of Sikhs in Delhi.

Sikh temples were set alight, priests guarding holy books were torched. Anyone who wore a turban was attacked. To save their lives the vastly outnumbered Sikhs cut their hair, but they were butchered anyway. The Indian Army, which could have prevented the killings, was confined to barracks by a government now under Rajiv Gandhi's control, while the only Indian general who had ever taken the surrender of an enemy army was called a traitor because he was a Sikh, his wife and children forced to flee their home to seek sanctuary with shocked strangers.

I accompanied a Sikh woman to the Delhi suburb of Trilokpuri, which had seen some of the worst carnage. Mistaking me for a member of the dead Prime Minister's family, people sidled up to me and proudly boasted how many defenceless Sikh families they had killed in their homes.

'How did you know where they lived?'

'We were given lists with their addresses. And cans of kerosene.'

'By whom?'

'You know. Everybody knows.'

They could not understand my rage. They certainly would not have understood the rage of the Indians flooding into a privately run relief camp with food and clothing for the wounded women and children who had survived the killings, where priests of every faith were trying to comfort the bereaved families, people of every religion trying to alleviate their anguish. All around me I heard the incandescent fury of ordinary Indians that the ruling party had kept the Army in barracks, claiming the massacre was a spontaneous outpouring of enraged grief. If this was true, they asked, why were so few Sikhs attacked in states which were not governed by Mrs Gandhi's party? Later they would ask why Rajiv Gandhi as Prime Minister would not hold an enquiry into the slayings, despite the detailed case-histories assembled by a citizens' committee headed by a Chief Justice.

Still, with Mrs Gandhi's assassination and the civil war in the Punjab it seemed no leader would, in the sinister understatement used in India, 'play the religious card' again.

We had forgotten Kashmir.

Nestled below the holy Himalayas, Kashmir possessed a unique religious mysticism. Kashmir's Islam was inspired by the ecstatic visions of the Sufi poet-saints; her Hinduism was a product of the great sage Shankaracharya, who had urged pilgrims to travel India from the beaches on the

Indian Ocean to her highest mountain-caves and learn they belonged to a common world. Indeed, during the carnage of Partition Mahatma Gandhi had described peaceful Kashmir as 'an island of sanity'.

But shortly before her death Indira Gandhi had dismissed its democratically elected government and installed a puppet government. Three years later Rajiv Gandhi did the same and the beautiful Kashmir Valley erupted in violence, convinced that it would never get justice from an imperialist Delhi. Demagogic priests played upon the insecurities of a largely Muslim population and Kashmir's mysticism was replaced by fantacism. Those who did not believe in Islam were terrorized out of the valley. The Army was sent in. Soon a hundred thousand Hindu refugees were eking out a miserable existence in camps, waiting to return to their homes. Twenty thousand Muslims could never return, killed in police and Army action.

As if the deadly adventurism in the Punjab and Kashmir was not enough, we now learned that Indira Gandhi had been financing and training Sri Lanka's Tamil insurgents to gain the support of India's thirty million Tamil voters, angry over injustices to Sri Lankan Tamils.

Under Rajiv Gandhi that training intensified. Sri Lankan guerrilla leaders were received in Delhi as guests of the Indian Government. India violated Sri Lankan airspace to drop supplies to beleaguered Tamils. Finally, an intimidated Sri Lanka invited India to dismantle the insurrection, but when our Army reached Sri Lanka it discovered that the rebels it had trained didn't want to be dismantled. During the next three years fifteen hundred Indian soldiers would be killed by Tamil guerrillas before a new Prime Minister, V. P. Singh, finally brought our demoralized troops home, leaving behind a festering Tamil hatred of India's leaders.

Punjab, Kashmir, Tamil guerrillas. So much damage unleashed in five short years – and the worst was yet to come.

Years ago, while conducting the negotiations for partitioning of the subcontinent, Lord Wavell, Viceroy of India, had observed, 'The more I see of these Indian politicans the more I despair of India.'

Now Indians themselves would despair of their politicians as the genie of Hindu–Muslim hatred was once again released into mainstream Indian politics.

In 1985 the Supreme Court of India granted an illiterate Muslim woman maintenance payments for herself and her children from the husband who had divorced her. The landmark judgement applied to all Indian women. But in 1986, to win the support of fundamentalist Muslim voters, Rajiv Gandhi used his brute majority in Parliament to pass a new law. Henceforth Muslim women would be subject to medieval interpretations of the shariat, Islamic religious law on marriage and divorce.

Moderate Muslim opinion and the vast majority of Indians were appalled. If the votes of Muslim fundamentalists were to be bought in this fashion, what would fundamentalist Hindus demand? Had the Prime Minister forgotten that the Hindu Laws of Manu sanctioned untouchability? Couldn't he see that naked opportunism was setting the cause of equality before the law back by centuries in India? Where would this end?

That question was answered within weeks in the small northern temple town of Ayodhya.

Many Hindus believe Ayodhya to be the birthplace of the god-king Rama, and it is ringed with temples claiming to be the site of the god-king's birth. Among the temples is a single sixteenth century mosque identified by some Hindu fundamentalists as the actual site of Rama's birth. To prevent religious disputes the mosque had been padlocked for half a century. Now angered Hindu fundamentalists prevailed upon a district judge to open the monument for worship to Hindus.

Suddenly remembering that Indian Hindus outnumbered Indian Muslims by six to one, Rajiv Gandhi permitted the fundamentalist Hindus to lay a foundation stone for a temple in the disputed precincts. Then he arrived at the mosque to launch his campaign for a new general election by promising to give India 'Ram Rajya', the government of the god-king Rama.

Only a Marxist had the courage to observe drily that India needed latrines more than India needed temples or mosques. The wise observation was ignored.

Seizing the political weapon which had so carelessly been placed in their hands, the Hindu nationalist party, the BJP, claimed to be the only party who could give India the government of Rama. Still, Rajiv Gandhi lost the general election, the Hindu nationalists didn't win it either, and India gained a brief respite when a new government threw a police cordon around the town and jailed religious rabble-rousers.

But the barred Hindu fanatics kept the issue of the temple simmering, their rhetoric becoming increasingly violent as a new general election approached.

And the Hindu nationalist party of the BJP grew steadily more powerful as it made the temple the central plank of its election campaign. Vowing to destroy the mosque and build a great Hindu temple on its ruins, BJP leaders toured the subcontinent exhorting every Hindu village in India to fire a brick for the new Rama temple, telling Hindus that Muslims profaned their faith.

Campaigning in the next election Rajiv Gandhi was blown up by a Tamil woman guerrilla wired as a human bomb.

India's new Prime Minister, heading a minority government, did not want to alienate the Hindu nationalists. The BJP were now the second largest party in Parliament.

Reassured by Prime Minister Rao's inactivity, one December morning in 1992 a mob of three hundred thousand Hindu fanatics, in the presence of BJP leaders, demolished the mosque with their bare hands, planting images of Rama in the rubble.

Massive Hindu–Muslim riots followed. Twelve hundred kilometres away from the mosque, armed groups claiming to be from the Shiv Sena, the BJP's closest political allies, began massacring Muslims across the length and breadth of Maharashtra state, insisting they were Pakistani spies. For a week the state capital, Bombay city, the engine of India's economy, shut down in fear. Within a month Bombay would shut down again as ten bombs exploded simultaneously across the city, damaging luxury hotels, corporate offices, the century-old Stock Exchange, killing and injuring hundreds.

How could this happen? Only fifteen years earlier, during the Emergency, I had seen the BJP leaders standing shoulder to shoulder with Muslim priests in India's largest mosque urging us to bring democracy back to India.

'Why are you engaged in this insanity?' I asked one of those leaders now.

'We are just doing what the Congress Party does,' she replied. 'But we are doing it better.'

Very much better. They had drawn up a list of other mosques which had to be destroyed.

Indeed, one of their followers, P. N. Oak, founder and president of the Institute for Rewriting Indian History, had written a whole book to prove another Muslim monument was built over a Hindu place of worship. He was circulating his book in the United States. His claim had even caught the attention of the *New York Times* and his supporters were clamouring to be heard.

The Taj Mahal, they said, was an affront to the Hindu faith. It must also be pulled down.

Twenty-Four

Stamping

During an election in the eighties a young woman, Nalini Singh, happened to be at a polling booth when the voting was suddenly disrupted by armed men. Brandishing their weapons to disperse the frightened voters, the men stamped the ballot-papers and at gunpoint forced the election official to seal the ballot-boxes.

The young woman was so appalled by what she had seen she decided to make a television film so the whole of India could watch their electoral system being hijacked.

In her film the director interviewed the gangs hired by political parties of every persuasion to make sure their candidates won. Masking their faces to hide their identities, the gangsters told the interviewer how they provided what they proudly referred to as 'the muscle power' of Indian politics.

First they bribed the villagers. If that didn't work they slapped the village elders around. If beating up respected members of the community didn't work then limbs were broken – an arm here, a leg there. If that didn't work, a gang member said with mock ruefulness, the odd voter had to be shot. But if the villagers or the factory workers or the slum dwellers still insisted on exercising their franchise then there was always the bomb, which made a big impression on the confidence of the voters.

To guarantee a sweeping majority for their boss, the gang members also captured whole polling booths and stamped every ballot-paper with their candidate's symbol – in the manner which had moved the director to make the film in the first place. When she asked the gang members if they were not afraid of the law they laughed.

The police, the bureaucrats, the judges were all hired by the state. And their candidate would be in control of state power. Who would dare to punish them?

Of course, many gang leaders have found it more convenient to enter politics personally. With their 'muscle power' they can guarantee victory and keep the spoils of the system for themselves.

Twenty-Five

The Greatest Show on Earth

After the heady euphoria of seeing the communist bloc countries throw off the shackles of the Soviet Empire, the world is discovering that the combination of political freedom and economic scarcity is a lot more dangerous than any amount of Molotov cocktails. Commentators wring their hands as they contemplate the potentially explosive situation in Eastern Europe, where all those longed-for freedoms are facing all those empty stores.

But for fifty years in India those dangerous freedoms have been maintained by millions of people with empty bellies who know each election is a poker game being played for the highest stakes – their future.

So there was great interest in the country in 1989 when the Union of India went to the polls for its ninth general election. The suddenness of the announcement and the speed with which the election was to take place – the bare minimum of time allowed by the Indian constitution – were calculated to ensure that the ruling government would be returned to power. Furthermore, believing the young to be partial to himself, Prime Minister Rajiv

Gandhi had recently lowered the voting age from twenty-one years to eighteen years. As a result, in this election half a billion voters were to exercise their franchise.

Five hundred million voters. Visualize every voter in the USA and Canada added to every voter in Eastern Europe and Western Europe – voting simultaneously in all their different languages to elect a common government. Then think of the physical enormities of putting such a huge electoral machine into operation.

Three weeks before an election, candidates must file their nomination papers and receive their political symbols. Symbols are a necessity in India, where half the electorate can neither read nor write and votes by recognizing a picture. Often a political party will put up an outsider with no chance of winning just so his symbol is confused with the symbol of a powerful opponent by people unaccustomed to looking at small images printed on paper.

Once the nominations have been filed only twenty-one days remain before polling. Now the Election Commission must print the papers. A seemingly easy task? Not in India. The Election Commission must get the names and symbols of all the candidates correct on half a billion ballot papers – in seventeen different languages, each with individual scripts. Then the ballot-papers must be conveyed to the vast number of polling booths across the nation, one booth for every thousand voters – from the inaccessible mountains of Ladakh on the very borders of Tibet to the farthest desert areas of Rajasthan on the borders of Pakistan to the southern coasts of Kerala on the edge of the Indian Ocean.

As political consciousness grows so does the number of candidates, and in this election a bemused television announcer showed a ballot-paper from a single constituency that had the names of one hundred and twenty-two different candidates printed next to their one hundred and twenty-two pictorial symbols. The actual ballot-paper was the size of a newspaper page and the announcer demonstrated that it took more than three minutes to fold the ballot-paper and insert it inside a box.

While the Election Commission is dealing with these logistical nightmares the campaigning begins in earnest. And campaigning in the Indian general election is political theatre of the craziest dimensions.

Songs. Street plays. Video films. Poets introducing candidates with specially composed odes. Campaign vehicles turned with mad invention into motorized chariots inspired by mythology. Personal appearances by miracle-workers and godmen, film stars and priests. Bazaar jingles satirizing the claims of the contestants. Massive political meetings attended by half a million people, door-to-door canvassing for individual votes.

The sheer force of the Indian electoral process has introduced a new word into the dictionary of democracy – Wave – to describe such a furious display of voter preference that it sweeps all calculation before it.

But to sceptics the word Wave suggests an electorate which can be duped. As Malcolm Muggeridge said, a man who can barely feed himself is not a man who can be politically conscious. So those millions of illiterate and starving voters who produce a Wave must in fact constitute a mob, capable of being manipulated through populist propaganda or intimidated through the use of force.

To examine populism first. In the 1950s market penetration was thought to be the best way of getting a message to the people. At that time the Coca-Cola company led the field in Indian market penetration and our Government invited Coca-Cola to distribute contraceptives along with their soft drinks. But villagers who needed to walk twenty miles to reach drinking water were hardly in a position to buy the paradise promised with the purchase of fizzy drinks, and the project was aborted. Once again government radio became the instrument of preaching population control.

By the seventies television had made its entrance into the Indian political arena. Like the radio, Indian television – this mighty weapon of communication – was controlled by government. But for the first time both were now used for political ends.

In 1975 Indira Gandhi declared a State of Emergency and embarked on a programme of mass sterilization of the male population. To compensate the sterilized individuals for their pain, their outraged dignity and their frequent sepsis, they were each given a transistor radio. On television and over those cynically awarded transistor radios the Indian masses were bombarded with a propaganda barrage telling them how wonderful things were under the benevolent reign of Mrs Gandhi and her family.

Knowing every voice of dissent had been silenced, this illiterate and frightened mob tuned their radio dials to the BBC World Service. As a result they were better informed than their Government. And when the Government finally called a general election in 1977 these same illiterate voters threw it out of power with a massive Wave.

But they had not elected an effective government. India's first experiment with a non-Congress government crumbled, and the voter turned once again to Indira Gandhi. Unsure of the electorate's loyalty, practising a politics fought with its back to the wall, she undermined the elected government of the Punjab, and that ill-advised action eventually cost Mrs Gandhi her life.

Still, Rajiv Gandhi looked like the beginning of a new politics. A pleasant and harmless young man who smiled a lot and showed great interest in computer technology, he promised to cleanse Indian politics of corruption and take India into the twenty-first century. He even acquired the sobriquet of India's Mr Clean. Riding a wave of sympathy after his mother's assassination, in 1984 Rajiv Gandhi won the most massive electoral mandate in Indian history.

Now India had at its disposal electronic communications. A country that sorely lacked drinking water was given satellite dishes to link a medieval culture to an electronic market-place, and the staggering power of this new form of market penetration was used to market a single product – Rajiv Gandhi and the virtues of his Government.

In living colour, we were entering the age of disco democracy. Think of the following panaceas offered to a country with India's problems by her Prime Minister in the years leading up to the elections.

American Presidents jog. So the Prime Minister of India instructs his cabinet to get into jogging suits. Mostly comprised of fat, middle-aged party bosses, the Indian cabinet is no ideal of physical beauty. But at least their traditional garments, evolved over centuries to accentuate the positive, disguise their more unaesthetic contours. Now they are required to put on grey jogging suits. Led by their Prime Minister to the theme song from *Chariots of Fire* blaring over loudspeakers wired to lamp-posts, they unhappily run around the main streets of the capital – their exertions beamed by television across the nation.

An astonished India asks – why are the men who control

our destiny dressed in this peculiar way? And what are they running from?

Earlier the nation watches an even more bizarre event. Rajiv Gandhi decides to re-enact Mahatma Gandhi's famous Salt March, though it is more a Salt Stroll, as it only lasts for the short duration of the photo-opportunities necessary for television. And far from being non-violent, it bristles with a special security force raised by the Prime Minister himself: Black Cat commandos in black leather boots and black fatigues and chic black berets and sub-machine guns, followed by convoys of security men and political groupies shouting slogans in praise of their leader – whose government is still taxing salt as the British Empire had done.

Here was proof of an entire government's faith in Macluhan's claim – the medium is the message. After all, half the Indian electorate cannot read or write. Half the Indian electorate is unable to earn one meal a day. How can it distinguish between the medium in which information is conveyed and the accuracy of the information being conveyed?

Television spectaculars proved not enough to preserve the massive mandate Rajiv Gandhi had received only five years ago. India's Mr Clean was seen as presiding over a politics of corruption unprecedented in a nation that thought it had witnessed every form of venality. There was even widespread belief that Rajiv Gandhi and his wife had robbed the Indian exchequer of millions in defence kickbacks during the purchase of the Swedish-made Bofors gun. His own Defence Minister, V. P. Singh, resigned in disgust to lead the fight against Gandhi's government.

Now Mahatma Gandhi's grandson entered politics to contest Rajiv Gandhi's seat. Though sharing a name, they were in no way related, as the pacifist Rajmohan Gandhi discovered in a baptism of fire from Prime Minister Gandhi's organizers when his workers were beaten up, his election agent took six bullets in the stomach, and his supporters' polling booths were captured. But then, the pacifist hadn't understood that India was up for grabs.

There appeared to be no over-riding issue that defined this election. No Emergency to end. No warring coalition to be dismissed. No sympathy to be expressed. As for corruption, India had grown weary witnessing the cupidity of her leaders. So in this, India's ninth general election, political personalities, journalists, pollsters, tea-shop pundits were asking the same question: would there be another Wave?

But the voter was keeping his cards close to his chest until polling day. Well, not every voter. Some voters put up posters, saying: *Wanted! Member of Parliament! Missing for Five Years.*

Others were even more explicit. A minister was canvassing his constituency, surrounded for reasons of status by gun-toting security police and television crews. Aware of the cameras on him, the minister stopped at a village and graciously invited a young man through the security cordon. The young man – a poor farmer – waited politely as the cabinet minister recited a string of election promises.

'And so I ask for your help,' the minister ended with an assured smile. 'Vote for me.'

'Five years ago I voted for you,' the young farmer replied, smiling shyly at the minister. 'But you were very busy and could not return from Delhi to look into our problems. So I borrowed money to buy a railway ticket and travelled hundreds of miles to see you. When I got to your house I told your guards I would wait as long as necessary to meet you. You were my Member of Parliament. You had promised I could come to you for help. After many hours you finally sent me a message. You did not want to see me. And your guards were to slap me for daring to disturb you. Now you have come to me, asking for my help. And I am giving you the same answer.'

In full view of the Indian press the young man slapped the minister across the face, daring, if only for a brief moment, to demand accountability before security guards descended on him.

'The sheer might of India's democracy stirs the blood,' the *Economist* magazine wrote when the election results were declared. 'The average Indian earns less than $25 a month and likelier than not is unable to read. This did not stop the country's half a billion voters from standing up squarely to their political masters – who between elections lord it over them and often steal from them – uttering one defiant NO after another.'

And what a NO this was. With the single exception of Bengal every governing party – state and centre – was swept out of power. And the Indian voter provided a resounding answer to the excesses of a brute majority by giving no party a majority.

In his first address to the newly elected Parliament the new Indian Prime Minister, V. P. Singh, acknowledged: 'The people of India have forced us to recognize the heterogeneous nature of our country. In creating a situation where political parties must depend on each other for support and govern by consensus, the Indian voter has demanded that politics in India change from the politics of personality to the politics of issue.'

The Indian voter got his wish. At the next general election the issue would be class war. The one after it would be fought on the issue of religion. Each time the electorate would deny political power not just to those who claimed the mantle of inherited power but to a new breed of political demagogues.

In fact for ten years the voter would refuse any political party a majority. But while the voter was displaying his displeasure with those in power, the inattentive Indian politician was acquiring the assets of power and indulging in the politics of real estate.

Especially in Delhi – where politicians routinely demand palatial government properties as their due for having once held public office and where even the city centre has been renamed, although the city's planning instructions state expressly, 'the names of existing streets should not be changed. The renaming of streets not only creates confusion for post offices and the public but also deprives people of a sense of history'.

On the other hand, renaming streets has the advantage of allowing politicians to rewrite history. So government residences are requisitioned for family memorials; monuments, airports, parks renamed; public money channelled into private family trusts; national institutions used to provide lifetime sinecures for politicians' relatives. Rajiv Gandhi even ingeniously made the budget of India into a family monument, so that government subsidies to agriculture are now permanently attributed to Nehru, welfare schemes for the poorest sectors of society to Indira Gandhi, youth employment and educational projects to Rajiv Gandhi – converting the citizen's own money into the politician's gift.

Seeing our highest leadership set the fashion, cities all over the country are now littered with familiar places bearing unfamiliar names belonging to politicians yearning for immortality.

But while our politicians protect themselves against their own impermanence with their self-serving memorials, the country's permanence depends on the continued existence of the Indian Parliament, designed by its British architect as a circle to contain all of India's warring aspirations within its embrace.

India has already faced two threats that should have destroyed that Parliament more effectively than any bomb placed under its foundations. Political totalitarianism, when all democratic process was suspended. Civil war, when religious sectarianism was unleashed.

Yet in the Punjab at the very height of the troubles, when they were being urged by their political and religious leaders to kill each other, Hindu and Sikh farmers did not do so. Their restraint made it possible for the Punjab to have peace again.

And a High Court judge, a man whose position and salary depended on government, had the courage to confront the most powerful person in India and find Prime Minister Indira Gandhi guilty of electoral corruption. During the trial, when every imaginable pressure was being brought to bear on him, from money to intimidation, Justice Sinha repeatedly told the Prime Minister not to perjure herself, and informed a courtroom crowded with sycophants and security personnel that they were not to jump to their feet when the Prime Minister entered the witness box.

'In this courtroom,' he noted severely, 'you may only rise for the law.'

In the years since Justice Sinha's judgment, the combined

pressure exerted by Indian society has slowly changed Indian politics and the results are beginning to show.

Today the Supreme Court is sentencing leaders across the political spectrum on corruption charges – Prime Ministers, members of the cabinet, leaders of all the largest political parties.

Today the Election Commission of India has finally banned the passing of populist bills on the eve of an election, and government media can no longer be used for political propaganda.

Today India's two hundred million lower castes have their own political party and are impressively represented in other political parties.

Today the authorities are enforcing a fundamental principle enshrined in our constitution – that the rhetoric of religious hatred is an illegal use of the political process.

Ironically, there is no problem that has arisen in other democracies – many of them older and richer than India – which India has not struggled to surmount. Sectarianism, affirmative action, political assassination, civil war, unstable coalitions, the electronic marketing of political aspirants, separatism, corruption.

The wonder is that India still exists to surmount them. And not only Indians think so. Commenting on the Indian general election of 1996, an editorial in the *Financial Times* of London noted, 'The democracy of India is a wonder of the world.'

And its guardian is not the politician so beloved of feature writers but the faceless, nameless, all-enduring Indian voter.

FOUR

Twenty-Seven

Getting There

As the pace of India's exchanges with the outside world accelerates there is a growing demand both inside India and abroad for some comprehensible definition of what India actually is. Definitions are hard to come by, but there are some great descriptions.

When Mark Twain visited India at the end of the nineteenth century he wrote of the delirium he hoped would never leave him when he saw

> ... the land of dreams and romance, of fabulous wealth and fabulous poverty, of splendour and rags, of palaces and hovels, of famine and pestilence, of genii and giants and Aladdin lamps, of tigers and elephants, the cobra and the jungle, the country of a hundred nations and a hundred tongues, of a thousand religions and two million gods, cradle of the human race, birthplace of human speech, mother of history, grandmother of legend, great-grandmother of tradition, whose yesterdays bear date with the mouldering antiquities of the rest of the nations –

the sole country under the sun that is endowed with imperishable interest for alien prince and alien peasant, for lettered and ignorant, wise and fool, rich and poor, bond and free, the one land *all* men desire to see, and having seen once, by even a glimpse, would not give that glimpse for the shows of all the rest of the globe combined.

More modestly, India has traditionally described herself as Karma Bhoomi, the Land of Experience, where everything has happened so often before that even history is reduced to troublesome echoes in an empty cave. But no experience in the Land of Experience, nothing in all her yesterdays, has equipped her for a world where her faith in the encompassing unity of life is in daily, even hourly collision with the explosion of fragmented information coming from outside.

Dismissing the possibility of ever defining India, in 1945 the writer Alex Aronson noted ascerbically that India was a civilization, and 'civilization is always a process: not a being but a becoming.'

Half a century later that observation still proves astute. Somehow India has managed to stay a civilization, still unpredictable, still surprising, still defying definition. Maybe India's indolence preserves her. Or her traditional fascination with unifying what appears fragmented. In any case, in a world of perpetual motion India remains a perpetual becoming, a vast and protean sea of human improvisations on the great dance of time.

Twenty-Seven

Reading

'Sahib! Latest from Plato, *The Republic*! Also, James Hadley Chase. P.G. Wodehouse. You want *Catcher in the Rye*, sahib? *Mad* magazine? But, sahib, just now unpacked. At least sample *Little Dorrit* by Charles Dickens.'

Learning to read in India meant hearing its pleasures shouted at you by pavement booksellers before you even knew how to read. It meant watching the animation on the faces of grown-ups bending over volumes displayed on threadbare scraps of carpet while the booksellers slapped another two books together to loosen the dust kicked up by passing pedestrians, cyclists, cars before whispering conspiratorially, '*Anna Karenina*, sahib. *Madame Bovary*. Hot books, sahib, only this minute arrived. Believe it or not, tomorrow no copies remaining.'

Surely there was no other country in the world where booksellers jumped onto the steps of moving trains, clinging with one hand to the iron bars of a window, and with the other pushed forward a cane basket brimming with books – cajoling, exhorting, begging you to read. Or where the ability to read was thought synonymous with a longing to read.

In a country where illiteracy is so widespread, the capacity to read is treated with a respect bordering on awe, and maidservants who could neither read nor write made sure that we steered our way past the alphabet into those boring reader's primers that described English schoolchildren named Janet and John endlessly running or jumping. Their glee in our achievements increased as our reading improved and we were able to repay them for the stories we had learned while sitting on their laps – tales of gods and warrior kings and manipulative ascetics who had cheated their way into immortality – with stories from our books of sleeping beauties and frog princes and the extraordinary adventures of Tom Thumb. Because of them the world of the imagination was opened to us, becoming as tangible as the corporeal world, as tangible as the next book waiting to be read by torchlight under the covers when they sent us to bed. And the act of reading became a pleasure so intense that adults often treated it as a vice when they could not draw us from our books to eat or bathe.

However contradictory adults were about our reading habits, they were consistent in demanding respect for the book itself. To deface a book was unthinkable. To put your feet on a book – container of knowledge and thought – was considered an act of such grossness it provoked the contempt of the entire household.

Reading was for us a significant part of the comfort of childhood, indeed a necessary comfort when we were sent off as infants to boarding-schools while our parents struggled for India's independence. In darkened dormitories with the monsoon rain beating so heavily on the tin roof it almost drowned our sobs of homesickness, we could be tricked from our loneliness by the teacher's voice reading tales of Harry the Horse and citizens who played games of chance; or the fortunes of Mrs Bennett's daughters; or Mehitabel signing off to her cockroach with the inspiring sentiment, '*Toujours gai*, Archie. *Toujours gai!*'

When we got home from school there were always more books waiting as gifts. Bought by others, not chosen by ourselves, these books carried an aura of duty. Fortunately, relatives paying morning calls on our parents would sometimes circle our heads with crisp rupee notes to remove the evil eye, pressing the money between our fingers. Now with cash in hand we were in a position to buy our own books, and the purchase of two books could enable you to read a hundred, thanks to the lending library.

But these were not the lending libraries of the First World. These were secret, shifting Indian libraries which fitted into garishly painted tin trunks small enough to be strapped onto the backs of bicycles ridden by librarians, who were usually clerks moonlighting from government offices. And their locations were only learned about through word of mouth.

Our favourite library took up three rungs on the wrought-iron fire-escape behind O. N. Mukherjee's Emporium in Calcutta. My *aficionado* elder brother assured me it contained the finest collection of Westerns in the whole world. By investing a fraction of a rupee and including some of your own books in the corpus of the library, you could borrow as many Louis L'Amours and Zane Greys as you could stomach. Or two-in-ones by lesser-known writers featuring a picture of an Apache on one cover, and when you turned the book around and upside down, a picture of a mounted cowboy with blazing six-guns on the other. Sometimes, thanks to the librarian's definition of a Western, you might find a Jack London or a Stephen Crane, and by this happy mistake be drawn into the worlds of other writers of action – Joseph Conrad, Alexandre Dumas, Leo Tolstoy.

Or opposite the Chinese shoemaker there would appear, with miraculous suddenness, the librarian who specialized in murder mysteries and Russian classics, heavily subsidized for the Indian market by the Soviet Union, so that reading Georges Simenon, Agatha Christie, Rex Stout was for us a natural corollary to reading Chekhov, Dostoevski, Gorki.

If this meant our tastes were formed by such books as the librarians could buy in second-hand bookshops, it also meant we were uninhibited by literary snobbisms, holding an unshakeable belief that any book we borrowed was a potential source of delight and – more important – that there did not exist the book too difficult to read.

The only obstacle to our reading appetites was the tragic absence of a lending library for comics. Alas, the steely-eyed owners of comic shops demanded full payment, Cash Down. Such hard-heartedness had enabled them to have permanent establishments – wooden shacks where they sat cross-legged on floors covered with white sheets, smirking at their hoard of treasure. Leaving our shoes on the road-side we would climb barefoot up the two steps leading into their shops and lose ourselves in a brave new world peopled by Superman, Batman, Scrooge McDuck, Archie and Veronica, Nyoka the Jungle Girl. And of course, those Classic Illustrated Comics which would later prove invaluable in getting university degrees in literature because the plots and characters of the West's great novels had been painlessly but indelibly engraved on our brains.

As we grew older, we did of course go to proper book-shops such as the Oxford University Press Book Store on Calcutta's main shopping avenue, Park Street, around the corner from Macaulay's home. The proximity was appropriate. Macaulay had persuaded the British Government to allow Indians to learn English so that they could become clerks for the British Raj. Leaving the blaring car horns and humidity of Park Street outside, we would enter the cathedral-like store with its glass-fronted bookcases made of rich, polished mahogany, manned by spectacled assistants whose hushed voices were barely audible over the hum of air-conditioning, and timidly ask for books.

Or in Delhi we would wander through the stucco pillars of Lutyens's Connaught Place searching for Ramakrishna and Sons until suddenly, hidden behind the sweeping colonial façades, we would locate a store piled to the ceiling with tottering pillars of books and an owner who knew where every title could be found and always had the book you wanted. Or we would browse in Faqir Chand's store in Khan Market because the hunchback owner never let you leave without a monogrammed ball-point pen or letter-opener even if you hadn't bought a book.

In Bombay, beyond the brooding Indo-Saracenic buildings of Bombay University, the Strand Book Stall had a policy of kindness to college students, and a credit line could always be negotiated while advertising executives bought their copies of *Catch 22*.

In these bookstores we struck intellectual attitudes, anxiously awaiting the four new Penguin titles which arrived every month and studying on other Penguins the author photographs of Katherine Anne Porter, Vladimir Nabokov, Nancy Mitford, Evelyn Waugh. Sometimes we abandoned our orange-coloured Penguins for the poets published in Faber and Faber's yellow paperbacks, or clutched the brightly coloured American editions of Gertrude Stein, Kerouac, Capote, Nathanael West, which could be so effectively colour co-ordinated with one's clothes.

Still, our passion for reading was not born in such establishments to visible self-improvement but in those pavement bookstalls and lending libraries which so tenaciously offered themselves as a necessary adjunct to every pleasure. If you were taken to a restaurant you had to spend long minutes examining the books spread in front of the entrance. As you did after you had seen a movie. Or been to a cricket match. Or illegally bought a packet of cigarettes. Thus were we made gluttons for books.

The same gluttony informs my reading today, and I remain as indiscriminate now as I was in my childhood. Give me a history or a biography and it will trigger off hours of rumination on human behaviour. A contemporary novel to keep in touch with the *Zeitgeist*. A golden oldie because each re-reading increases an original passion for the book. Give me a volume of poetry for that kidney punch, what Emily Dickinson called 'that turning to ice of the limbs' so essential to the compulsive reader. Or a book on science or philosophy, since who can tell when one might suddenly grasp the Theory of Chaos or Kierkegaard. And give me always a couple of detective novels in case my flight is delayed.

I admit it. I am an addict. Addicted to reading by those pavement magicians shouting at us like circus barkers, those booksellers endlessly rearranging their displays as they corrupted us with their seductive litany of titles, luring us away from the little world of the self into whole galaxies of the imagination.

Twenty-Nine

Indian Décor

At the beginning of this century a young Indian Lancer from the kingdom of Jodhpur who had fought against the troops of the Dowager Empress of China in the Boxer Rebellion took some time off for rest and recreation and visited Japan. As he was of noble blood he was received by the Emperor of Japan at the palace in Kyoto.

The Lancer was horrified by the austerity of the ruler of the Chrysanthemum Throne. 'Except for a painted screen at the very end of the audience chamber,' the Lancer noted in his diary, 'the audience hall was completely EMPTY.'

Such shock on the part of an Indian would have been entirely appropriate, according to William Archer. The British Indologist describes the Indian aesthetic as being one of 'gargantuan excess'. So the Lancer might well have understood the zen principle behind the Emperor of Japan's décor, since zen is a corruption of the Sanskrit word *dhyan*, meaning awareness. But to achieve awareness through the contemplation of a solitary object amounts to tunnel vision for an Indian.

Not for India the tranquillity of gazing at the glaze on a single perfect pot. We find satisfaction in the glazes on a hundred different pots, in a hundred stages of disintegration. What the West hides in the attic to be examined in moments of nostalgia, Indians keep proudly to hand. On the wall of an Indian home a miniature painted in the sixteenth century by a master artist to the court of a Moghul emperor will hang next to a group photograph taken to commemorate a meeting with a minor British official during the days of the British Raj, and both will fade into obscurity against the lurid colours of an Indian calendar with its illustrations of voluptuous Indian deities or film stars.

While this makes the Indian home interesting it also means that the Indian home is without a 'look' and fails to 'make a statement', lacking the discrimination which in Europe and America constitutes an aesthetic.

But then Ananda Coomaraswamy, the great scribe of Indian culture, is scathing about aesthetics. He dismisses aesthetes as mere effetes, capable only of the passive response. And there is no passivity in the Indian home. It dares to exist in a civilization where eras and cultures are colliding with such force that the home itself is only sustained by an act of will, clinging stubbornly to an idea of order in the midst of disorder, a gallant belief in form in the midst of malfunction.

I once overheard a French lady commiserating with a former Maharajah as he showed her around his palace. 'You must be so sad to see it like this,' she said sympathetically. 'It must have been formidable when it was perfect.' Her host looked bewildered – he simply did not understand the sentiment. The Indian home has never been perfect. It is always in a state of decay and re-assembly.

And in this mobility lies the essential difference between excess in India and excess in the West.

For a start, mobility in the West is directed upwards. Increased status and wealth confer the capacity and the necessity for visible improvement, demanding that residences, objects, furniture, paintings become ever more refined, more exclusive. In short, discrimination is all. But Indians are short of cash. They cannot afford to remake the world closer to the heart's desire. In contrast to the upward mobility of the West, the Indian home has a sort of amoebic mobility capable of assimilating both an individual history and the history of a civilization which, because it cannot afford to throw things away, absorbs them. Or waits for them to fall apart.

The Indian's home is neither his castle nor a stage set by his decorator. By necessity it is organic. So travellers to India will be familiar with high-ceilinged rooms that still retain the iron hoops from another century which once held heavy curtains attached by ropes to small boys in adjacent chambers pulling the curtains to stir the summer air. Today, between these hoops there hangs a fan with wide wooden blades where a family of sparrows is nesting – because the noisy air-conditioner listing at an awkward angle beneath a carved window has long since rendered both iron hoops and wooden fans obsolete.

If the Indian home has an aesthetic it is chaos, enabling it to accommodate regional influences as separate in their ways as Spain is from Scandinavia, as well as European influences from the long reign of the British Empire and Islamic influences from eight centures of Muslim domination. So an average Indian bungalow, for instance, will probably have a pillared verandah: the number of pillars outside a Hindu home traditionally indicates the eminence of the owner. Well, it did until the British imported the aesthetic of Grecian and Roman pillars. Now in your average bungalow, European decoration and Hindu tradition are fused in stucco to support a roof from which is suspended the traditional Indian swing, facing wrought-iron lawn furniture derived from the European gazebo. Above the pseudo-Palladian doorway hangs a garland of holy basil leaves and marigold blossoms to bless the house, and on the un-Indian architrave is precariously balanced an image of the elephant-headed God of Protection, Ganesh.

Inside the rooms, woollen or silk carpets with Persian motifs will – if it is winter – lie on top of cotton durries used in spring, and both are removed during the summer heat to reveal stone or marble floors. Such attention to the ground is inevitable in a culture accustomed to taking off its shoes before entering a room. Then on the carpets will be a heady variety of furniture – from the bolster-covered platforms on which Indians habitually recline, to the Victorian sofas and chairs on which Englishmen once sat bolt upright, to the Art Deco and Art Nouveau remnants from the days when Indians danced the tango.

Enclosed corridors and walled courtyards indicate the influence of Islam's sequestered women, and in the dining room – a British concept – silver or copper platters, with individual food containers as dictated by Hinduism's caste considerations, lie in happy juxtaposition to assorted items of European china.

Over time the architecture and artefacts of alien worlds have been made familiar to India through extended usage. Possessions are not so much displayed as lurking around, waiting to be used – in themselves incontrovertible evidence that when an irresistible force such as life meets any immovable object, something's got to give. In India that something is usually good taste.

So it is no good asking an Indian, 'What is that refrigerator doing, plugged into that marble wall inlaid with cornelian and lapis lazuli?'

Because the Indian will only look at you as though you are a cretin and answer, 'Keeping the water cold.'

It was India's greatest film-maker who summed it all up. Satyajit Ray once said that Indians have an infinite tolerance for decay. Certainly in our homes elements of heart-stopping beauty co-exist with examples of equally heart-stopping awfulness. While such intolerable tolerance occasions distress in the visitor it seems to leave the locals curiously unfazed. Perhaps this is because the Indian looks on his home more as a place to live than as a work of art. The art, if there is one in India, is supposed to lie in the living.

Thirty

Filming

The year India became a free country the Indian film-maker Satyajit Ray helped found the Calcutta Film Society. In later years he would celebrate Calcutta, often associated only with beggars and infamous black holes, as Mahanagar, the Great City.

Not that Ray had an easy time filming his celluloid poems of the great city's anguished humanity. Politicians objected when Ray's films were cleared by the film censor. 'He is painting a bad picture of the nation,' they complained. 'The world will think we have only poverty.'

The politicans needn't have worried. The world wasn't interested. Western distributors found Ray's films too slow and Indian distributors declined to show them because 'people come to see films in order to forget their problems. Who wants to see reality on the screen?'

It is true that in avoiding reality Indian cinema audiences have created the largest film industry in the world, most of it based in Bombay, a city which has taken to calling itself with awful coyness Bollywood. And Bollywood has given its audiences escape in every form – from religious

epics to emotional melodrama to action movies affection-
ately known as curry Westerns to ghost stories, all filled
with the song and dance routines which are an essential
part of commercial Indian cinema.

But an industry that learned its craft from the Lumiere
brothers themselves, when the men who invented cinema-
tography visited India at the turn of the century, has
addressed both reality and fantasy in its hundred years
of existence. True, the first Indian feature films made by
Dadasaheb Phalke had mythological themes; *Rajah
Harishchandra* in 1913, *The Legend of Krishna* in 1918.
But they were designed to make audiences gasp at miraculous moving pictures that could so suspend reality you
could see gods flying high above human beings.

The fact that they were silent transcended the barrier of
India's many languages and India's common mythology
freed the film-maker to use all the magic of the new technology to make his audiences marvel at film's possibilities.

A common mythology has been indispensable to the
growth of our cinema. Indian movies have been described
as India's folk plays transferred onto celluloid, since both
have a familiar array of stock characters, music and dance
routines, and plots that mix tragedy with comedy. This
formula has allowed films to penetrate into the deepest
corners of India, making an alien medium only another
vehicle for the familiar.

So in the twenties and thirties, while some Indian
directors shot lavish spectaculars and even used foreign
actors and European locations, other directors, watched
closely by the administrators of the British Raj, used the
narrative form of folk drama and seemingly innocuous
themes such as the life of the great singer saint Meera-bai,
or the heroic King Prithiv Raj, to make thinly disguised

political allegories for an audience fired by nationalist fervour.

When India became free, directors dealing with uncommercial subjects such as money-lending or the poverty of Indian farmers still managed to make films of powerful social commentary like *Mother India* and *Do Bigha Zameen* into block-buster successes both at home and abroad. At the same time Indian cinema was turning out popular comedies and melodramas, using some of India's most talented musicians and singers to compose film scores and record songs to which actors mouthed the words.

But commercial cinema's dance routines were perforce becoming a little more suggestive. Dance choreographers had to compensate for the ban on kissing on film, imposed by the puritans of the new India. Our film censors had made it official. Kissing was un-Indian.

From the late sixties onwards India was awash in undeclared money, and cash fortunes found their way into the film industry as a convenient form of money-laundering, dictating its new vulgarity. Stars who could pull in an audience were earning huge amounts of money, acting in three or four films simultaneously, rushing from one shoot to another with ever larger entourages. It was the heyday of the curry Western, the superstar, the lush location. Dance sequences which began in the valleys of Kashmir suddenly included an Eiffel Tower or a Trevi Fountain around which the hero and heroine issued their voluptuous invitations to each other, although one memorable dance sequence confined itself to the keys of a huge red typewriter.

By the time the industry entered the eighties our films were unselfconsciously ripping off American television serials and flaunting the special effects of wealth. It was no longer wrong to be be young, beautiful, Westernized and bad. Skirts and sequinned gowns appeared on the ladies, leather jackets on the gents. Stars spent more time on motor bikes, helicopters, speedboats and less time in the Indian countryside where eighty per cent of their audience lived. And hit movies were made or broken by the suggestiveness of their dance routines, leaving us all longing for the simple days when a kiss was just a kiss, not this piston-like movement of hips and breasts by fully clothed members of opposing sexes. In Parliament they had hardly noticed that Indian film stars were kissing again. The country's representatives were now trying to control the dancing.

During these two decades, films from a new wave of directors bridged the gap between the fantasies of commercial cinema and the daily events of ordinary Indian lives, funded by a newly created government film finance board.

But one group of young film-makers from Kerala wanted to avoid accepting government largesse with its inevitable corollary, government interference. This left them with the problem of raising on their own the seemingly impossible sums required to pay for film stock, actors, cameras, cameramen, lights, sound men, costumes, sets, laboratories, editing studios.

For weeks they debated the best means of funding their film projects. Finally they came up with the novel notion of screening films in villages for a fee. Hiring a van and a projector they sent out word to the Kerala villages that they would be holding film shows for which they would make the nominal charge of one rupee, the equivalent of three cents. The excited population of whole villages crowded into rice fields for the great event. The cinema was actually coming to them, at a price even they could afford.

'How long did it take to earn the finance for your film?' I asked one of the directors, Adoor Gopalakrishanan, at a festival where his film was being shown.

'About a year and a half.'

'That's all? Did you expect to do it so quickly?'

'We kept our costs low and rented movies from the film societies.'

'What did you make those poor villagers watch?'

'Eisenstein and de Sica. Resnais. Pabst. Kurosawa.'

We both knew that most of the villagers at the screenings had never been to a town, let alone seen any pictures of the outside world. Now they were being forced to sit through those lengthy film classics, shot in black and white.

'Did they like anything?'

'Of course. Why not? Indian villagers can understand the story of *The Seven Samurai* better than you or me. They enjoyed *Bicycle Thieves* also. Only they hated *Hiroshima Mon Amour*. Catcalls and boos, I'm afraid.'

Hiroshima Mon Amour. I tried to visualize all that French world-weariness being projected in an open field with no electricity for miles around – with cattle lowing and pi-dogs barking – for the delight of a village audience.

'Did they have a favourite?'

'We gave many repeat performances of Eisenstein's *Battleship Potemkin*. If you ask me, their taste is better than the audience at this film festival.'

His story reminded me of Louis Malle's experience while filming in Calcutta. Malle had been inspired to make a series of documentaries on India after seeing the documentary film of India made by Rossellini in the fifties. A friend of mine, Santi Choudhary, who had been Satyajit Ray's partner for several years but now had his own film production company, was working with Louis Malle.

Malle's filming was halted one day by a huge demonstration against the Government. Passions were running high and the crowds were expected to swell to half a million people. The police had put out radio bulletins advising people to stay in their homes, not to attend their offices, in fact not to venture out at all unless they had urgent business.

Determined to capture this event on film, Malle prevailed upon Santi to take him to the Maidan, Calcutta's central park, where the demonstration was to take place. Warning Malle the crowds would turn hostile if they saw cameras and sound equipment, somehow Santi manoeuvred the film van into the centre of the demonstration. As Santi had predicted, when tanned Frenchmen wearing safari suits and loaded with film equipment began exiting the van, an agitated Calcutta traffic policeman pushed his way towards them, gesticulating wildly.

'Get away! Go. please! Big strike! Unsafe! Bad for foreigner!'

Santi heaved himself out of the van and whispered conspiratorially into the policeman's ear. 'Can't you let us stay? This is the great French film-maker Louis Malle.'

The cynical ploy worked better than he had expected. The traffic policeman clapped his hands in delight. 'Louis Malle? Louis Malle himself? But I have seen his films and read all about him in *Cahiers du Cinéma*. Please translate. Ask what he personally thinks of the work of Jean-Luc Godard.'

As Santi pointed out later, if the traffic policeman's facility with language wasn't up to conversing with Louis

Malle in English, how had he ever managed to understand *Cahiers du Cinéma*? That bible of cineastes was only published in French. The policeman probably had a salary of forty dollars a month, but he told Santi he had somehow scraped enough money together to become a member of the Calcutta Film Society. Now here he was in the middle of a Calcutta demonstration, described by international journalists as among the most potentially violent situations in the world, happily discussing the minutiae of French New Wave cinema with a French director.

But then, as Satyajit Ray has shown the world through his films, Calcutta is the Mahanagar, the Great City – whose citizens manage to dream under the most oppressive conditions. And as the traffic policeman proves, their dreams are not necessarily the dreams that come out of the fantasy factories of Bollywood.

Maybe that is why they reacted as they did when a tearful radio announcer told his city that their ailing film-maker, Satyajit Ray, had died. People poured out of their homes. Offices closed down. The Government was brought to a standstill as bureaucrats deserted their desks.

During his lifetime this giant of the cinema always had to beg for money to make his next film. In a career spanning forty years, budget limitations seldom allowed him to film more than two takes of any scene, no matter how complicated, forcing him to draw each frame of his film scripts meticulously by hand so that he could shoot in a series of single takes. He composed the music, wrote the dialogue, designed the sets, directed the action, edited the rushes for films like *Mahanagar* and the *Apu Trilogy* and *Charulata* and *The Music Room*. When they were screened at film festivals around the world, he was acknowledged as a master of his form. But distributors and film financiers in India were adamant. 'Your films will only lose money. We want films that give Indians the chance to escape the drudgery of their lives.'

Before his own government honoured him he was honoured many times abroad, and even as he lay dying in hospital the President of France awarded him France's Légion d'Honneur and Hollywood, not Bollywood, gave him a lifetime achievement award for his contribution to cinema.

Yet India's distributors called him a financial loser, his work of interest to the very few. They said they knew their audience. Did they? Learning of his death, in a spontaneous display of grief six hundred thousand people came out on the streets of Calcutta to pay silent homage to Satyajit Ray as his body was driven to its cremation.

Has any audience anywhere in the world given any filmmaker such an accolade?

Thirty-One

Communications

One Sunday morning in 1996, I was glancing through an Indian newspaper and chanced upon a mirror of contemporary India. The following stories were adjacent on the front page.

A telecommunications company had just concluded its negotiations and was in a position to offer Indians who owned personal computers a facility to access web sites in two hundred and thirty countries. This was quite handy, as Indians had begun placing matrimonial advertisements in the electronic marketplace.

No longer limited to the Indian Sunday newspapers, now readers around the world could respond to

Government Contractor Builder seeks alliance fair beautiful sharp-featured girl from educated, status family. Correspond with bio-data

Or *Compatible Bride wanted for Associate Professor. Early decent marriage*

Or *Foreign Qualified Architect invites alliance from slim fair charming modest soft-spoken well-mannered adjustable-natured sitar-playing sociable humorous cultural broad-minded honest loyal with clean past conversational English preferably architect or civil engineer bride.*

Luckily for his future bride this demanding bridegroom had added *Religion Caste Faith No Bar.*

There has been a dramatic change in matrimonial demands in the last few years. Fewer advertisements require the same caste or religious faith, or object to previous marriages. The essential requirements for both sexes seem to be professional and educational qualifications. And a large number of advertisements are from people with MBA degrees from Western universities who are living abroad. In fact, the newspaper columns are now headlined by professional status: *Doctors, Civil Servants, MBA/CA, Non-Resident Indians, Other Foreigners.* So it is common to find advertisements for

Wanted Beautiful Vegetarian Convented Medico Match for Smart Handsome MD Radio-Diagnosis No Bars

Or *American white male 35 years sincere honest looks for Indian wife*

Or *Distinguished Decorated Handsome Army Captain seeks Convent-Educated Wife Serving Army Doctors Preferred: Caste, Widow No Bar.*

The willingness to marry widows is particularly poignant because the next column in the newspaper carried an article on *Sati* – the vile practice of Hindu widows burning themselves alive on their husbands' funeral pyres.

Although *sati* has been illegal in India for nearly two centuries, in 1987 in the western Indian state of Rajasthan an eighteen-year-old widow who had been married only eight months committed suicide by burning herself on her husband's funeral pyre in full view of her whole village and thousands of spectators from nearby villages. The local authorities had looked the other way on the grounds that they could not have prevented it.

'After all, she was a Rajput girl,' they said.

There was indeed a historical tradition of Rajput women burning themselves on their husbands' pyres, especially when a battle had been lost and they stood the chance of being taken prisoners. They were treated as saints for their act of devotion. Their cenotaphs were places of pilgrimage, mostly to other women desperate to give their husbands sons. In fact, the young widow had burned herself on a pyre next to the cenotaphs of three earlier *satis* of the village.

The authorities had hoped, rather too optimistically, that the whole sorry business of this modern *sati* would remain a local secret. But the story of a new saint spread like wildfire, drawing legions of pilgrims who required soft drinks, souvenirs, food, garlands of flowers and incense to place at the spot where the *sati* had burned herself, the opportunity of hearing accounts of her life from people who knew her when she was a mere mortal, accounts of miracles witnessed since she became immortal.

Local politicians rushed to the spot, eager for self-promotion. Some argued that such acts of heroism symbolized all that placed the Rajput woman so far above her Indian sisters. Others wanted the officials, the woman's family and the watching villagers all tried as accessories to murder.

Journalists and women's rights groups descended on the village from all over India. Can you imagine that her act of *sati* was voluntary? the women's groups shouted. Even if she went willingly she was only a young girl trying to escape the cruelties still practised against rural widows, forced to cut off their hair, living like slaves on the charity of their in-laws.

I knew what they meant. I had once travelled in a railway carriage filled with young women with shorn heads, their bare shoulders and shins exposed by saris once white but now grey with coal-dust from the engines. They looked like children with their long, vulnerable necks, these village widows on their way to Benares to cover their shoulders with cotton scarves printed with the prayer Hari Krishna Hari Ram, which they would recite for their dead husbands as they begged in the streets until they themselves died of starvation.

Meanwhile the journalists were asking: Had the woman been forced into burning herself by the avarice of her husband's family, trying to earn a supplementary income from the spectators and sightseers? Or was it a plot in which all the villagers were involved? Would other village women be forced to do the same thing?

A reporter who had visited the area told me she had interviewed the village women. 'I was quite surprised. When I enquired if any of them were also likely to commit *sati*, they said, "Only if our husbands agree to burn themselves on our funeral pyres if we die first." '

Under the glare of the entire nation's attentions the local authorities panicked and had the building of a temple stopped, forbidding the villagers from any further exploitation of the young widow's death.

Now, ten years later, an enterprising young reporter had decided to revisit the area just to see how things had progressed. He found people still placing flower garlands on the site of the immolation. Television antennae waved above the village huts. This struck the journalist as particularly horrible. He was convinced an ancient and cruel practice had taken this village into the world of global communications, and the revenues from that practice were keeping the village there.

Between the two articles on web sites and *sati* was a picture of a young man with ear-rings and shoulder-length hair.

The accompanying story informed us that a young Indian rock star had arrived in town from London, and the music he was playing to packed halls was a hybrid of Western and Eastern tunes called Indi-pop. The photograph made him look like a native American warrior. But we were told there was already an Indi-pop star called Apache Indian. Or was he a Raga-rap star? Still, the ear-rings framing the singer's clean features and strong brown face were similar to those worn by many Indian farmers. Perhaps he should have been playing Bhangra-rock, that other Indian music craze which combined the insistent drumbeats of a northern harvest dance with the equally insistent beat of rock and roll.

Anyway, there was no reason for him to be self-conscious about his appearance. The audience of young girls dancing to his music were themselves dressed in hybrid forms – saris and mini-skirts, anklets and Doc Marten boots, *salwar kameezes* and torn Levi's – enjoying a brief fling with freedom before the restrictions of Indian society overwhelmed their lives.

One of the songs such audiences had already made into a huge hit had the evocatively Indian name 'Arranged Marriage'.

Thirty-One

Trees

In India when a boy and girl get engaged, their horoscopes are read by the family priest to see if the couple are compatible. But astrological compatibility extends far beyond whether the young man and the young woman will suit each other. The priests of India are supremely uninterested as to whether Darby finds his Joan or Abelard his Heloïse. They are searching for the wider significance of the union.

'When this girl marries into our family,' the bride-groom's parents ask their priests, 'will she bring us luck? Will she increase our wealth or will she cast a shadow over our house, perhaps shortening her mother-in-law's life or bringing bad health to her father-in-law?'

If the girl's horoscope reveals the faintest hint of such possibilities the priests shake their heads and inform the prospective in-laws, 'It is very sad, but you have chosen a *manglik* girl to be your son's wife.'

Happily for the *manglik* girl she is not doomed by a fate over which she has no control to the life of a frustrated spinster. There is a solution to her problem. She must first marry someone else, transferring her ill-fortune to another husband. Then, purified, she can finally marry her bridegroom secure in the knowledge that she is bringing to his house only good luck.

But which husband is so noble that he will marry this unfortunate girl first, and take upon himself her ill-starred destiny, only to release her, cleansed, into the arms of another man? Travellers in India will have passed trees with withered flower garlands hanging from their branches. Those garlands denote the presence of a husband. The *manglik* girl garlands a tree as her bridegroom in a marriage ceremony as elaborate as that between human beings – to cleanse herself of the misfortunes of her fate. And of course, if it is the bridegroom who is the *manglik* then he takes a tree as his first wife.

The use of trees to receive evil is an idea as old as India itself. The devout still believe the tree is all that remains on earth of the sacred Soma plant which provides nourishment to the gods themselves. The Atharva Veda, written a thousand years before the birth of Christ, contains the prayer

The sin, the pollution
Whatever we have done with evil
With your leaves we wipe it off.

Is it any wonder that the tree is sacred to India? Or the forest a *tirth*, a place of pilgrimage as holy as any temple?

To the artists of India the tree has an even greater significance. They believe the tree gifted art to mankind. The Puranas, the texts of the oldest Indian legends, tell the story thus: the gods had become quarrelsome and Vac, Sacred Speech, fled the profaning gods to hide in water. When the vengeful gods claimed her, the intimidated waters gave her up. So Sacred Speech fled the waters and took sanctuary in a forest. Again the gods claimed her, but the trees refused to surrender her to the spiteful gods. Instead the trees gave Vac to man in offerings made of wood: the flute, the drum, the lute, the pen. With these men were instructed to tell of the Creation.

Then there is the tree and Indian philosophy. To the philosophers of ancient India the forest was the symbol of an idealized cosmos. The great Indian philosophical academies were all held in groves of trees – an acknowledgement that the forest, self-sufficient, endlessly regenerative, combined in itself the diversity and the harmony which was the aspiration, the goal of Indian metaphysics. It is not by chance that out of India's forests came the great body of India's knowledge: the Puranas, the Vedas, the Upanishads, the epics of *The Mahabharata* and *The Ramayana*, the Yoga sutras and the medical studies of the Ayurveda.

Inevitably, such veneration of the forest had its impact on the city. Following the geometry of Indian philosophy, the Indian city had at its heart a grove of trees from which the streets emanated outwards like branches – to remind the city-dweller that man is only one part of a enormous living organism. And when the city-dwellers had fulfilled their obligations to the material life of the city – marriage, children, governance, war, trade, pleasure – they retreated to the forest to end their lives in contemplation and meditation, drawing from trees the tranquillity necessary to such reflection.

Again, it is not by chance that the Buddha and Mahavira, the founders of Buddhism and Jainism, two of India's great religions, should both have attained enlightenment not on the road to some Damascus but while meditating under a tree.

The Indian Nobel Prize Laureate, the poet Rabindranth Tagore, attempted to explain the essential silvi-culture of India in his book, *Tapovan*:

> Indian civilization has been distinctive in locating its source of regeneration, material and intellectual, in the forest not the city. India's best ideas have come when man was in communion with trees. Indian thinkers were surrounded by and linked to the life of the forest, and the intimate relationship between human life and living nature became the source of their knowledge.

It is as if, over thousands of years, India has woven a mantle of conservation around herself with threads of morality, art, philosophy, religion, mythology. Especially mythology.

Trees feature in so much Indian mythology – providing shade or sanctuary to the divine – that they have become sacred in themselves. The goddess Meenakshi resides in the forest at Madurai, a grove sacred twice over because it is also the playground of the god Krishna and his adoring milkmaids. In Kanchi, the god Shiva, creator and destroyer of worlds, once appeared to a sage sitting under a mango tree. That mango grove became a pilgrimage centre; all mango trees have been considered sacred since.

Throughout India trees are worshipped as incarnations of the goddess. Bamani, Rupeshwari, Vandurga are the divinities who reveal themselves to men in the guise of such trees as the saal, the deodar, the banyan. And the goddess Aranyani, goddess of the forest, has inspired a whole body of texts known as Aranyani Sanskriti, which translates as 'the civilization of the forest'.

That civilization was founded by India's first inhabitants and it is still followed by their descendants. In tribal India the tree is venerated as the earth-mother, not only because trees provide food, air, nourishment, occupation, materials for housing and fodder and fuel, but because without the tree there is neither soil nor water: nothing to prevent the one from being washed away, the other from evaporating. In the great tribal tracts of India – home to the Bhils, the Santals, the Nagas, the Bishnois – whenever a child is born a tree is planted in the child's name, forging a relationship between child and tree closer than that between child and family because that tree is uniquely the child's. The trees are all slow-growing, and by the time the child reaches adolescence his tree has just come into fruit, beginning its life as provider to the tribal and the tribal's life as guardian of the tree.

The forest, then, is India's central metaphor for the Creation, venerated as a symbol of inexhaustible fertility, represented again and again in Indian art as the tree of life, referred to again and again in Indian literature as a paradigm of the cosmos.

So, with all this veneration, this adoration, this reproduction in art, literature and philosophy, it seems beyond belief that Indians could have permitted half the trees of India to be cut down by the administrators of the British Empire in the last century to make way for railways and mines, and then themselves cut down half of the remaining half during the last thirty years.

The Hindu scriptures tell us that we are living in Kalyug, the Age of Evil, the era of immorality. And the characteristic evil of our evil age is speed. Even so, the statistics of what is happening to the subcontinent's forest cover are shocking proof of the velocity of our immorality.

Of the thousands of miles of dense virgin jungle that covered the great range of the Nepal Himalayas as recently as 1950, it is calculated that if commercial felling continues at the present rate there will not be a single tree left by the end of the century.

Logging and stone-quarrying have destroyed the forest cover of the Indian Himalayas with equal devastation. We know the impact this is having on the monsoon rains, which are life or death to the subcontinent, and yet we watch complacently while the denuding of the Himalayan forests leads to a cycle of flood, drought, homelessness and hunger which repeats itself with increasing speed as our glaciers retreat and our topsoil is washed away and our waters evaporate because there is nothing to retain them.

And each year we see the price of our indifference exacted from the rice fields of Bangladesh as swollen rivers burst their banks with such frequency the world is now inured to the thought that each year in Bangladesh another half a million people will lose their lands, their livelihoods, some even their lives.

By replacing veneration of the tree with consumption of the tree it is as if the subcontinent is no longer able to connect cause with effect.

The sages sitting in the forests of ancient India reciting the Puranas may have had some presentiment of the India that was to come. The Puranic legend says the marauding gods were enraged when the forest refused to surrender Sacred Speech to them and gave her instead to man as instruments of music and literature. In their anger the gods placed a fearful curse upon all trees: *'Because through instruments of wood you have given what is sacred to mankind, so again with instruments made of your bodies, with axes with wooden handles, as thunderbolts will men cut you down.'*

Nearly three hundred years ago men and women of the Bishnoi tribe died in an attempt to end that curse. The Bishnoi faith prohibits the cutting of green trees and demands absolute protection for the khejari, the shade and fodder tree of the area. As a result their lands are still fertile while all around them fields have been reclaimed by the Thar desert of Rajasthan. Although in earlier centuries other members of the Bishnoi tribe gave their lives to protect their trees, the story most often told describes the martyrdom of Amrita Devi — a woman from a Bishnoi village in the kingdom of Jodhpur.

Amrita Devi, like her fellow tribals, had been raised to love and tend the trees that encircled her village. So when the axemen of the Jodhpur king — needing timber for the royal lime-kilns — arrived to chop down the trees, Amrita Devi confronted the axemen and begged them to leave the forest untouched. She explained the religious beliefs of the Bishnois. The king's axemen were unmoved. As they unsheathed their axes Amrita Devi flung her arms around the first tree marked for felling. The axes of the soldiers sliced through her body and as she bled to death she uttered the words which have become a slogan of her tribe. 'A chopped head is still easier to replace than a chopped tree.'

Then Amrita Devi's daughter took the place of her dismembered mother. She too was killed, only to be replaced by a younger sister who, in dying, yielded her place to the third and youngest sister, who also gave her life trying to protect the tree with her body. Throughout that day unarmed men, women, children from eighty-three surrounding Bishnoi villages converged on Amrita Devi's village to protect the trees, but the axemen continued relentlessly to fell the trees and their protectors. By nightfall nearly four hundred tribals from separate Bishnoi villages had been butchered. Like Amrita Devi and her daughters, whole families had died in defence of the khejari forest.

There is an annual fair still held in commemoration of those deaths in Amrita Devi's village. A regular visitor to this fair is a man named Sunderlal Bahuguna, whom many Indians revere as 'the Mahatma of India's Forests.' He calls the fair 'my one important place of pilgrimage' because it is the method first used by the Bishnoi tribe that he emulated in the Chipko movement to save what remains of the Himalayan forest.

The word *chipko* means to cling, and throughout the Himalayas villagers and conservationists, students and folk poets, are attempting to halt India's deforestation by clinging to trees marked for felling by commercial contractors. The Chipko movement is also planting trees, fighting to replace the monoculture forests of fast-growing trees – like the eucalyptus and the pine, intended for the wood-pulp industry, which give nothing to the soil or to the people who live off the soil – with the great slow-growing trees and the mixed forests on which so much of India's economy and ecological balance depend.

The movement has now spread from the Himalayas to South India, where ten years ago a group of peasants – men and women – marched *en masse* to a government nursery and uprooted thousands of eucalyptus seedlings, planting tamarind and mango seeds in their place, protesting that these trees, not the eucalyptus, keep the soil and its people alive. Of course they were thrown into jail, while Indian newspapers continued to carry full-page advertisements for just such government nurseries, heavily supported incidentally by the progressive officials of the World Bank, urging Indians to invest in eucalyptus.

Money Grows on Trees! the newspaper advertisements shrieked.

Earn Green Gold!

Sometimes trees were not mentioned at all, merely wealth.

Bumper Profits Will Be Yours!

The officials who run these nurseries, as indeed their colleagues in the World Bank, would not pass the test of good government described in a folk tale of the Santal tribes, who live in Bengal and Orissa.

Once upon a time, the tribal story goes, there was a king who had many water reservoirs, and around the edges of the water he planted trees: mangoes, peepuls, palm trees, banyan trees. And the banyan trees were bigger than any of the other trees. And every day after his bath the king used to walk about and look at the trees. And one morning as he did so he saw a maiden go up to a banyan tree and climb it, and as soon as she was safely in its branches the tree was carried up into the sky. But when the king went back to the same spot in the evening he saw the tree back in its place again.

The same thing happened three or four days in a row. The king told no one what he had seen, but one morning he climbed the banyan tree before the maiden appeared. When she clambered up its branches he was carried up to the sky along with the maiden.

In the sky the maiden descended from the tree and went to dance with a group of celestial milkmaids. So the king also got down and joined in the dance. He was so absorbed he took no notice of the time. And when at last he tore himself away he found the banyan tree had disappeared. There was nothing to be done but stay in the sky.

So he began to wander about heaven and soon he came to some men building a palace as quickly as they could. He asked for whom the palace was being built and the men said, 'For you. Because you are a good ruler who plants trees for your subjects so they will have food and shelter long after you have gone.' Suddenly the banyan tree reappeared, so the king climbed back into it and was carried safely back to earth.

After that the king used to visit the banyan tree every day, and when he found it did not wither – although it had been taken up to the sky by its roots – he concluded that what he had seen was true. He began to prepare for death, making no answer to the questions of his courtiers as he distributed all his wealth among his subjects. A few days later he died and was taken to the palace he had seen being built in the sky.

Because, it is said by us Santals, *the trees you have tended in this world will bring you honour in the next world and all the worlds beyond.*

I can't help agreeing with the Santals. Planting a tree does indeed bring honour to those who plant it – including all those politicians who plant trees with fixed smiles on their faces while the world's cameras record their exertions. But as an Indian I know there is more than honour in the act.

For us the preservation of trees is as much a matter of cultural as of ecological survival. The forests of India have been the cradle, the university, the monastery, the library of Indian civilization. By exchanging our essential love of the tree – which gave us a view of the world in which man and nature were dependent on each other – for a

Western culture which has made man the monarch and the consumer of nature, clearing forests first for agriculture and then for industry, we are exchanging our capacity to understand the relationship between living things for a purely linear, purely profit-oriented view of the world.

And for a more precise understanding of what such a view means to the world we have only to listen to the alarm expressed by the astronauts circling the globe. They tell us they can no longer see Earth from space. Our planet is now obscured by smoke from Siberia to Brazil, rising from the funeral pyres of our great forests.

India has traditionally prided herself on being Karma Bhoomi – the Land of Experience – dismissing other countries as the lands of the consumer. It is true that from the folk tales of her tribals to the monumental works which are the pillars of Indian civilization, India has no shortage of experience to help the world find a balance between man's technology and the earth on which he wields it.

But if the curse of the Puranas has found its time and Indians persist – like thunderbolts – in slaughtering their trees, then we will become a people ever more deracinated. We will, quite literally, cut ourselves off from our cultural and philosophical roots by the action of cutting down our trees.

Thirty-Two

Love Song of India

In the twelfth century the poet Jayadeva sang India's greatest love song outside the Jaganath Temple in the holy city of Puri so that passing strangers, forbidden entrance to the temple, could also listen to the trysts and deceptions, the separations and consummations, described in the *Gita Govinda*.

The temple of Jaganath is one of the holiest places of pilgrimage in India because it is home to the last benign incarnation of the god Vishnu. When this epoch is over Vishnu will incarnate into Kalki and destroy the world.

In possession of such a valuable treasure the priests of Jaganath are among the most ruthless in India. Only Hindus belonging to the higher castes may enter the temple. And yet Krishna, an earlier incarnation of Vishnu, is gained not by caste but by *bhakti*, the ecstatic love of God felt by devotees who hope to die with God's name on their lips. Pushing forward in the crush to touch the idol when the god is carried in procession through the streets of Puri, many devotees have been ground to death under the unstoppable momentum of the chariot's huge wooden wheels, thus giving the word juggernaut to the English language.

Now, standing before the Jaganath temple, where all could hear the *Gita Govinda*, Jayadeva sang of the milk-maid Radha's adoration for a beautiful young cowherd with a dark complexion and a perfect body, who plays haunting music on his flute and seduces every milkmaid, breaking Radha's heart even as he increases the intensity of her desire. The cowherd is the divine Krishna, and in erotic images of breath-taking sensuality Radha makes love to Krishna in Jayadeva's *Song of God*.

There is a stone slab in the dusty ground in front of the temple to commemorate that moment when low-caste Hindus, Muslims, Buddhists, Jains, who could not enter the temple, all listened to Jayadeva sing of Radha's longing for the adulterous Krishna in some of the most sublime poetry ever written. They heard Radha's aching request to her companion to find this god who came to her bed marked with scratches from the embraces of other women, and the constant refrain of her shameless plea, 'Oh friend, make him make love to me.'

They listened to the sexual desire that made her escape from her home to wander through the dangerous jungles of the night to keep a tryst with the god who did not come and did not come while she waited in a fever of longing and fear, and when he finally appeared his body was streaked with another woman's collyrium and sandalwood and he lied to her and still she trembled when he touched her.

Everyone who heard it became intoxicated by Jaya-deva's ecstasy, even the listening king of Puri, who traditionally paid temple girls to perform devotional dances and songs in the temple precincts. Now the intoxicated king decreed that the temple singers must sing the *Gita Govinda* at dawn and at dusk in the temple every day. The lord must be awakened by hearing this divine song. It must be the last sound the god heard before he slept.

The passionate love song spread through India like fire, adding a new dimension to the mythology of Krishna. Indian history is full of these *bhakti* movements, great waves of spiritual ecstasy that break the hold of social and religious exclusion to sweep every section of Indian society into the embrace of an all-inclusive passion. Poets and singers, lost in their ecstatic songs, have for century after century mobilized millions of people to break the boundaries of social separation. But nowhere has *bhakti* been so perfectly stated as in the *Gita Govinda* which Jayadeva sang in the holy city of Puri, expressing through Radha's lips his own longing for union with his god.

Eight centuries after Jayadeva sang his ecstasy to passing strangers I went to Jaganath temple, hoping to hear the temple singers sing his song when the god was put to sleep for the night, only to be told the temple trust had been taken over by the Government and there was no provision for singers any more.

Then a priest remembered the last of the temple singers was still around. After many messages of entreaty she reluctantly agreed to come to the temple and sing the *Gita Govinda* a final time.

At eleven o'clock that night I entered the temple and made my way past the mighty tower with its circling erotic sculptures into the main hall. It was a warm evening and people were sitting on the ground talking to each other or prostrating themselves or telling their beads, while children ran around with fresh flower garlands dangling from their fingers. Older people with austere features recited their mantras, holding in their laps leaves containing hibiscus and marigold blossoms and pieces of coconut as offerings for the gods. It was the usual combination of gregarious socializing and private worship that goes on in any Indian temple.

At the back of the hall I found an old woman of about seventy years with a broken leg, lying full length on her back, resting her head in her daughter's lap. The priest accompanying me whispered that this was the singer, but she was in such obvious discomfort I hesitated to disturb her and she acknowledged my greeting perfunctorily, turning her head away.

Hidden behind the huge doors which separated the inner sanctum from the main hall were the idols of the god and his family. While we waited for the doors to open I sat on the ground watching the children crawling around their mothers on the stone floor and thought about the temple tower outside, with its sculptures locked in blissful copulation, wondering why Indians are able to look at such sculptures without giggling but the most sophisticated Westerner, accustomed to pornographic television channels and sexually provocative advertisements, is overcome by self-consciousness. Was it the guiltless delight of the sculptures that made the visitor self-conscious?

A sudden clanging of bells interrupted my musing. The doors of the inner sanctum were flung open, and the gods were revealed – wooden idols with totemic shapes from India's original tribal culture which the new religions had not been able to subjugate, only to absorb.

In the presence of the gods the atmosphere in the hall became electric, charged with devotional intensity. People were singing and chanting prayers, their voices rising in a kind of urgency as they moved towards the railing that separated them from the sanctum. I saw the old temple singer limping forward. The priests cleared a space in the crowd so that she could face the gods. Hands folded, eyes closed, she began to sing. Her voice was cracked and unmelodious. She could not manage the exacting rhythm, the precision of expression, the changing ragas conveying different moods, required by the *Gita Govinda*.

The priests quickly lost interest in her attempt to send the god to bed with the sublime song soothing his dreams, and plunged the hall into darkness. The scent of burning camphor filled the hall. The old singer's voice petered out in confusion as the priests began circling the deities with their lamps and pressing food that had been first offered to the gods into the hands of the crowds mobbing them, swiftly seizing the money that was offered in exchange.

The singer limped out of the hall, leaning on her daughter's shoulder, obviously irritated at my romantic fantasies which had brought her out of the comfort of her home. As she grudgingly accepted the money I pressed into her fingers, I realized her irritation was justified.

In the reality of modern India, Indian sexuality is increasingly dictated by Western fashion, and the sensual and sexual confidence that created India's majestic erotic monuments has now been replaced by packaged fantasies.

Young Indians, given access to MTV and its Easternized versions when India opened up to cable television in 1990, have begun styling themselves on the sexual and romantic practices of the mean streets of America or Europe, while lower down the ladder of wealth, where the social mores of traditional Indian society deny easy intercourse between the sexes until after marriages arranged by parents, proliferating publications suggest the more urbanized the Indian the more repressed his sexuality.

A new phenomenon is spreading from India's smallest towns to her largest cities – sex by advertisement. In the last two or three years there has been a steady increase in new magazines with such names as *Broad-Minded* and *Pussy-Cat* which carry articles on Mother Teresa next to pages and pages and pages of advertisements from couples from all over India.

The advertisements are for group sex with strangers: *KGB secrecy assured/expected*

Introductions to the world of sex: *Do you wish to taste the forbidden fruit? Shy and reserved young girls welcome*

The longing for experience: *First Timer, Virgin, Very Lonely to be Loved, Having Unique Fantasies*

Or the frisson of safe adultery: *Are you a lonely housewife? I can arrange a broad-minded meeting place. Two housewives can jointly contact for mutual fun and enjoyment.*

We may be the land of the Kama Sutra, that great text on sexuality written by a celibate sage. We may have the Black Pagoda of Konarak with its twenty-foot high statues locked in consummation. We may worship Shiva in his phallic form and place garlands on the yoni of the goddess. But today we answer such advertisements as:

Well-educated, Mature Hygiene-Conscious Couple Broad-Minded Fun-loving, Interested to meet Ladies, Men, Couples. Should be Well Mannered, Decent. Strict Confy [confidence] Assured

Or *First Timer couple, She Bi, He Well Hung*

And promises, promises: *Baby It's your Lucky Day – Handsome Smart Guy – Terribly Exhausting.*

Come back, Jayadeva. India needs another *Gita Govinda*.

Can't you see the whole country is heaving, unfulfilled, telling strangers in magazines, 'Oh friend, make him make love to me'?

Thirty-Three

The Old Ways

Several thousand years ago the greatest sages in India, communicating with each other through their telepathic powers, agreed to consider the human condition. So they levitated to a cave in the Himalayas for a summit of wisdom and ended up producing the science known as the Ayurveda, the Knowledge of Life.

From their own lengthy meditations the sages of the Ayurveda had perceived that Time was Maya, the great play of illusions that disguised the eternal energy of the universe. They also knew that men feared time, because of all living things only humans were aware of their own mortality. Now the sages asked themselves how humans, in their constant state of agitated activity, could acquire the concentration to discover the universal life-force which alone could help them realize their eternal selves and cure their fear of time.

Put another way, how could men find the energy to be still? It is the paradox that informs every aspect of Indian thought, and over centuries many Indian disciplines have evolved to help mankind find the poise and balance necessary for stillness.

For the ear there is the recitation of mantras, or sacred syllables. Whatever religious significance is imputed to them, mantras are only a series of sounds and chanting them is an attempt to still the mind by constant repetition, a method that crosses over into Indian music which uses a single scale as its mantra, endlessly developing that scale to produce a meditative state that lifts both musician and audience beyond pleasure into contemplation.

For the eyes there are the mandalas, circular forms and representational figures, and there are the yantras, geometric patterns which purport to carry the secret codes of existence. Ignore their mystical claims and mandalas and yantras remain visual aids, created as a meditation for the eyes. Their patterns have found their way into Indian textiles and crafts. Their colours have defined the psychological states induced by Indian painting.

The entire body is the province of the science of yoga. The epigrams of the sage Patanjali identify *asanas*, or postures, in a system of physical disciplines designed to release energy. The last and greatest practice of yoga is controlled breathing, because breath is the origin of life. Those yogis who have mastered that discipline are able to slow down their breathing to such an extent it is almost death, eliminating the separation between man's concept of life and that which is always living.

The whole human being is the focus of the Ayurveda, which holds that human suffering takes three forms – physical, mental, spiritual. To alleviate the body's suffering Ayurveda has compiled a vast encyclopaedia of healing plants, many discovered by the original inhabitants of India's forests and mountains, her tribal population. For the suffering mind Ayurveda prescribes a variety of meditations to enable a patient to achieve harmony with himself and control his destructive restlessness. And for Ayurveda's final and greatest concern, the health of a man's soul, the sages state that no man can be free of suffering unless he understands the interdependence of all life.

To help man exist in the external world we have the Vastushastra, the body of Indian treatises on architecture. Vastu starts from the premise that the original act of architecture is the earth, home to all forms of life. When a house is built certain rituals must acknowledge this fact. The foundations of a house are an invasion of the earth and so the architect must place in the foundations seeds and roots to resow the earth. The raising of the house's central beam is commemorated with another ritual to remind man of a past in which the tree provided the support on which he placed leaves or skins to create his first microcosmic habitation on the wider habitation of earth.

The house's architecture must acknowledge those elements from which life is composed – earth, air, water, fire, energy. In its ideal construction it should be a series of buildings containing space, opening into a series of courtyards which are pure space in which the elements may move freely, as they do upon earth, and it should have a pavilion, containing space while still remaining space, to allow the energies of the earth's magnetic fields to enter from all sides. Instructions on the planting of gardens and trees, as well as the alignment of water bodies and the necessity to keep water and air free of pollution, treat the act of building as the creation of a living thing.

Mantras, mandalas, and yoga have always been used as routes to self-realization in India. Today Ayurveda and

Vastu are staging a vigorous comeback, a sign that Indians are at last acquiring the confidence to examine their own knowledge to find answers to their problems. Unfortunately much of the current interest in Vastu is based on a superstitious belief that a house which observes Vastu tenets can harness energies which will bring wealth or good fortune to the owner. And more and more books on Ayurveda are concerned with beauty aids, reducing a concept of the universe as a harmonious whole to the preoccupations of narcissism.

Even the contemplations which are supposed to lead to an understanding of the unifying principles of life are so often used selfishly that India's Nobel Laureate, the poet Rabindranth Tagore, raged, 'Alas my cheerless country, dressed in worn-out rags, loaded with decrepit wisdom. You pride yourself on having seen through the fraud of creation. Sitting idly in your corner, all you do is sharpen the edge of your metaphysical mumbo-jumbo . . .'

I think Tagore was a bit harsh, but our piecemeal practices of a unifying philosophy have indeed fragmented a once intact vision of the world in which man is the guardian of a living organism, responsible for seeing its fragile equilibrium is maintained. The result is all too visible. Modern India is a vast landscape of raucous disharmony. More than ancient sages explaining the nature of eternal unity, today India requires wise men to explain our current disharmonies, observers to explain our continued denial of what is living in favour of what is shining – and in the process perhaps provide a bridge between our past and our present.

I suppose the scholar G. V. Desani could be called a modern wise man. He certainly has the credentials. He spent fourteen years as an ascetic, travelling India, studying philosophy and performing rigorous physical disciplines to understand the connection between India's ancient knowledge and her present. When he found himself stranded in England during the Second World War, out of sheer homesickness he wrote his glorious novel, *All About H. Hatterr.*

Mr Hatterr is a bankrupt Eurasian living in Bombay whose friend Mr Banerji finally gets him a job on an Indian newspaper writing about various sages – the guru of Bombay, of Madras and so on. Each of the seven gurus Hatterr encounters, grown rich from the credulity of his followers, gives him a philosophical lesson on Living. Hatterr's attempts to apply these lessons to his own life lead to a great Adventure, taking him inadvertently towards an enlightenment which he describes to his friend Mr Bannerji:

'As to *Truth*, the great generalization is, *Dam mysterious!*'

Through the eyes of an amateur reporter, part-Asian, part-Western, in the centre of contemporary Indian chaos, Desani uses the most complicated schools of Indian philosophy to exhibit the Indian comedy – that play of illusions at the centre of her metaphysics. It is a brilliant feat of intellect, and to achieve it he has invented an Indian English of such energy that reviews by T. S. Eliot, Edmund Wilson and E. M. Forster expressed amazement and the British writer Angus Wilson described it as 'a Whole Language . . . like the English of Shakespeare'.

But the story continues – through the author. Returning to India with his reviews Desani, like his hero, tries to find employment writing for the magazine *The Illustrated Weekly*. The editor refuses to believe that he is admired by such distinguished literary figures as T. S. Eliot and suggests Desani has written his reviews himself. Upset that his veracity is in dispute, Desani retires into a concrete chamber and enters a yogic trance, lowering his metabolic rate until he is in a state of suspended death. Thus he remains until the editor makes an abject apology.

But then as Hatterr notes on the first page of his book:

WARNING!
Improbable, you say?
No, fellers.
All improbables are probable in India.

It is an incident worthy of the pen of the cartoonist Laxman, who records India for the national newspaper, the *Times of India.*

If India needs a contemporary account of the great play of Maya it need only look at Laxman's daily report on power to the nation. The politics of India have given Laxman a contemporary mythology as packed with overwhelming personalities, as elaborate, as full of colour and incident as the power struggles described in *The Mahabharata.* But our egalitarian times lack an epic grandeur so it is only fitting that they should be recorded by Laxman's common man.

With the startled look of someone who has chanced upon a theatrical performance, a bemused common man occupies the corner of every Laxman cartoon, observing the increasingly bizarre behaviour of India's public figures. From his vantage point he watches the machinations of megalomania to which its perpetrators are oblivious, his dazed expression puncturing the elaborate self-delusions of the human race better than the maxims of a sage.

The common man of Laxman's cartoons peoples the novels written by his brother, R. K. Narayan.

The Bachelor of Arts, Mr Sampath the Printer, The Financial Expert, The English Teacher, The Vendor of Sweets – the titles of Narayan's novels suggest their modest world in the small fictitious town of Malgudi, which is itself half village and half contemporary urban India, allowing Narayan to observe the collision between the two while creating a range of characters whose lives have chronicled the life of modern India.

In *The Guide*, a petty criminal escapes from jail and seeks sanctuary in a temple, pretending to be a holy man. When a drought occurs the villagers believe that only his holy powers can end it, and so they help him to fast until the rains come – Indian mendacity confronting Indian superstition in a struggle of life and death.

In *The Painter of Signs*, a simple man who prides himself on his calligraphy is hired to paint population awareness signs by a militant feminist from the city with whom he falls in love. His courtship of her provides an elegant display of the encounter between traditional and modern India. In *The World of Nagaraj*, a man who wishes only to write a great thesis on the paradoxes of the sage Narada finds that he cannot think because his nephew has married a girl who plays screeching Indian film music all day long in the hopes of becoming a playback singer in the movies. But which is the greater crime – vulgarity or withdrawal from the world to pursue the arcane?

It is our good fortune that two such gifted brothers should have happened to live in India during our first half-century of freedom, as if the gods knew we desperately required our own great satirist and our own great ironist to keep us sane. Their combined work could stand alone and still provide a record of India's first fifty years as an independent nation.

And the energy with which the philosopher, the cartoonist, the novelist have confronted modern India should dispel Tagore's fears of India's continued withdrawal from 'the fraud of creation'. The great thing is, their work also gives us a choice – withdrawal or participation. Now we have guides for both.

So I find my own suffering better alleviated by laughing every morning at Laxman's wry view of India than by contemplating my navel. But yoga makes my laughter last longer.

Graham Greene may say Narayan's work has offered him a second home but it has also made Indians more comfortable in theirs. If those homes are built by the methods of the Vastushastra, so much the better, but when the reality beyond the walls seems too jarring to be endured, Narayan's irony makes it tolerable.

And when mandalas and mantras and Ayurveda's herbal tonics all fail to cure the panic attacks induced by India's mounting chaos, we can always turn for solace to Hatterr's hard-won enlightenment.

Then his creator, G. V. Desani, yogi and thinker and teller of tales, instructs us to plunge recklessly back into the sea of India, cheering us on with the philosophical injunction:

Carry on, boys, and continue like hell.

Thirty-Four

The Shape of Things

In 1912, shortly before he received the Nobel Prize for Literature, Rabindranath Tagore was asked to write a poem honouring George V on his coronation as King Emperor of India. The irritated poet composed instead a hymn in praise of the God who was

> Supreme leader of the minds of all people,
> Ruler of India's destiny.
> Punjab, Sind, Gujarat, Maharashtra, Dravida, Orissa, Bengal,
> The Vindhyas, Himalayas, Jumna and Ganga,
> The waves of her swelling oceans
> Waken, taking your name,
> Asking your blessing,
> Singing your glory.

The hymn became the national anthem of a free India and years ago, when my son was only five years old he told me another story about gods and India. I have since tried to find out where he might have learned the story because he doesn't remember and no one else seems to know it. I have consulted Sanskrit scholars in Varanasi and have looked through books on Indian legends, but I haven't succeeded in finding its origins. Maybe the story is his own, a child's explanation of the birth of his country. Or maybe it is the interpretation he gave to his grandparents' determination to give him a country.

In any case the background to the story is this. Shiva is deep in meditation in an ice-locked cave in the Himalayas. The goddess who loves him has been banished from his sight lest she disturb his meditation. She wanders the world trying to forget the great ascetic, determined not even to turn and look in his direction. But she cannot help herself and standing on a wave in the Indian Ocean, she turns and stretches her arms towards the mountains, beseeching the ascetic god to enter her embrace. Into the space between her arms explode rice fields and deserts and rivers and stone fortresses and elephants and glaciers and coconut palms and temples – in short, the continent of India.

'That is why,' my son informed me, stretching his arms towards to me in the semaphore of embrace, 'India is this shape.'

Perhaps it needs a child to recognize there is a force pulling into itself every tragic disparity, every dispersion of race and language and religion, every confusion that is India, inspiring in its peoples a feeling larger than patriotism, something which they stretch out their arms to reach. Tagore called it a geography made sacred by devotion. I can't say what it is, only that when I am away it pulls at me, and I long for the land shaped by longing.

Thirty-Five

Leisure Activity

The word *firdauz* in Urdu means divine leisure. It is used to acknowledge the gift of something so unique only God could have crafted it when he had nothing else on his mind. And so we say, God made it at his leisure. The expression is sometimes used to describe:

The smell of the Indian evening – smoke from burning leaves mixing with the smoke of burning cow-dung and the incense of evening devotions

The scent of parched earth in the monsoon rains when peacocks fan their tails to dance

The green sweep of parakeets crossing the sunset

Kites wheeling in a becalmed sky

Pyramids of gaslights preceding a bridegroom seated on a white horse, and wedding bands playing 'A Summer Place' in march time

Drying saris spread along a river bank

The soothing shadow of rice fields at dusk

The harsh light of the desert and mica glittering in the sand

The sound of cowbells over car horns, the gentle eyes of Indian cows meandering through city streets until they sit down in the centre of the road in clumps and you know it is going to rain

The noise of crows at daybreak, the dew glistening on cobwebs

The clanging of bells in an Indian temple, the crying babies held on the hips of veiled women

The bell sounding from the neck of an elephant plodding down a city avenue

The ankle bells of a dancer

Film music blaring from tea stalls, the hypnotic litany of the street vendor

The solitary flute of the mountain goatherd haunting the empty hills

The steady drone of chanting monks around the tree where the Buddha reached enlightenment

The cry of the muezzin, There is no God but God, and the ecstatic singing of the quawaalis

The warning cough of the tiger, the cobra hissing in a basket

The popping of water lilies, the snarling of pi-dogs, the koyal bird crying for rain

Idols floating into the ocean, garlands disintegrating in the tide

The white horizon of the holy Himalayas

The shriek of the train whistle, coal-dust on wooden seats, a river crossing at night time

Jasmine and marigold garlands wet from a bucket of water.

Glass bangles sold by lantern light, fragile colour fracturing the dark

The rustle of starched muslin against the limbs, the warmth of stone floors under bare feet

The cooling of henna on the palm, the smoothness of brown skin under the hand

Spices stacked in triangles: orange turmeric, red chillies, grey cumin, black mustard seeds

The scents of Indian perfumes – attars of vetiver and sandalwood, of jasmine and opium, a drop of attar of roses made from a thousand petals of the thousand-petalled rose, and the attar called leisure

The smear of colour on a Hindu woman's forehead, the silver ornaments plaited into a Muslim girl's hair, the angular ear-rings in a tribal woman's earlobes, the bright turban on a northern Indian's head, the austere shawl on a southern Indian's shoulders, the muslin mask across a Jain monk's mouth, the saffron robe of the celibate, the matted locks of the ascetic

Bread swelling like a cloud on the platter, white rice steaming on the banana leaf, a yard of coffee cooling between steel glasses

A clay pot beading the hand with moisture, a bamboo spoon grazing the tongue

The village tank, the marble dome, the step well

An assembly of men pulling at hookahs between the taproots of a banyan tree, lanterns swaying from a bullock cart, the blaring horns of painted lorries

The stench of the Indian bazaar – flowers, incense, over-flowing gutters, petrol, dust, sticky sweets

The assault on the senses

The caress of the senses

Surely God made India at his leisure.

Political Chronology

1947
August 14/15, British Empire transfers power to the new
nations of India and Pakistan. East and West Pakistan
separated by land mass of India
British Empire announces details of partition awards
August–September, seven million people cross borders,
religious killings leave over a million dead

1947–1948
Integration of independent kingdoms into India and
Pakistan. Ruler of Kashmir joins India following invasion
by tribesmen from Pakistan. Pakistan retains invaded
territory. United Nations oversees Kashmir cease-fire line

1948
Mahatma Gandhi assassinated by Hindu fanatic

1950
Constitution of India adopted
Chinese troops enter Tibet

1951
First Indian general election. Jawaharlal Nehru returned as
   Prime Minister, leads National Congress to victory in
   three general elections
First Five Year Plan of economic development inaugurated

1959
State government of Kerala dismissed
China annexes Tibet, Dalai Lama takes sanctuary in India

1962
Indo-Chinese War on Tibetan frontiers
Chinese troops enter India through state of Assam

1964
Death of Nehru, Shastri new Prime Minister of India
Green Revolution in agriculture launched

1965
Indo-Pakistan War on two western fronts, Kutch and
   Kashmir

1966
Shashtri dies in Tashkent during Indo-Pakistan peace
   conference convened in the Soviet Union

1966
Nehru's daughter, Indira Gandhi – no relation of Mahatma
   Gandhi – appointed interim Prime Minister of India by
   National Congress

1969
National Congress splits into factions

1971

Fifth general election, Indira Gandhi wins landslide victory
with slogan Remove Poverty, changes party name to
Congress (Indira)

Revolt in East Pakistan, crack-down by Pakistan Army

Nearly ten million East Pakistan refugees cross into Indian
states of Assam and Bengal

Indo-Pakistan War

East Pakistan becomes nation of Bangladesh

1975

Justice Sinha of the Allahabad High Court finds Indira
Gandhi guilty of electoral malpractice

State of Emergency imposed on India

1977

General election; Janata Party wins, Morarji Desai becomes
Prime Minister

1979

General election called

Bhindranwale campaigns with Indira Gandhi's candidates

1980

Seventh general election, Indira Gandhi becomes Prime
Minister

Bhindranwale and his followers take up residence in Golden
Temple of Amritsar

Sanjay Gandhi crashes aircraft over capital and is killed

1981

Rajiv Gandhi elected Member of Parliament

1982
India begins arming of Sri Lankan Tamils

1984
State government of Kashmir replaced
Indian Army sent into Golden Temple
General election called
Indira Gandhi assassinated by Sikh guard, Rajiv Gandhi
    becomes acting Prime Minister
Sikhs attacked in Delhi, Government claims 2,300 Sikhs
    killed in two days, Citizens' Committee places figure at
    over 4,000
Rajiv Gandhi wins general election, becomes Prime Minister

1985
Supreme Court rules all wives are entitled to civil alimony
    for the maintenance of their children and themselves.

1986
Rajiv Gandhi government passes new law making Indian
    Muslim women subject to medieval interpretations of
    Islamic Shariat Law.

1987
India invades Sri Lankan airspace to drop supplies to Sri
    Lankan Tamils
Indo-Sri Lanka peace accord
Indian Army invited to Sri Lanka to disarm Tamil insurgents

1988
Disputed mosque at Ayodhya opened
Agitation begins for construction of Hindu temple at
    disputed site

1989

Foundation stone laid at Ayodhya for construction of Hindu temple

Ninth general election won by National Front coalition, V. P. Singh becomes Prime Minister

Indian Army brought back from Sri Lanka after 1,500 Indian soldiers killed fighting Tamil guerillas

1990

V. P. Singh enforces job and educational quotas for lower castes, riots follow

Hindu nationalist party, Bharatiya Janata Party, launches nation-wide agitation for building of temple at Ayodhya

Government puts security cordon around disputed site, jails agitators

1991

General election called

Rajiv Gandhi blown up by Tamil woman guerilla wired as a human bomb

Narasimha Rao becomes Prime Minister of minority Congress (Indira) government

Reform of Indian economy, tax structure

State elections in the Punjab

1992

Mosque at Ayodhya demolished, Hindu-Muslim riots follow

1993

Ten bombs explode across Bombay

1996
General election
BJP wins largest number of seats, but not enough to form
  government
Deve Gowda of Janata Dal party becomes Prime Minister,
  heading thirteen-party coalition
Accused in Sikh killings of 1984 sentenced, including
  ministers from Rajiv Gandhi government, compensation
  paid to victims' families
State elections in Kashmir
Senior political leaders and government officials face trial
  on corruption charges, many sentenced to jail

1997
I. K. Gujral of the Janata Dal party becomes Prime Minister
K. R. Naranayan of the most backward Indian caste becomes
  President of India
India celebrates fifty years as a sovereign democracy

Acknowledgements

Seven of these essays have appeared in different forms in the following places:

Channel Four Television, UK
House and Gardens magazine, US
London *Sunday Times* newspaper, UK
New Delhi magazine, India
The Pleasure of Reading, Bloomsbury Publishing, UK
Resurgence magazine, UK
FMR magazine, Italy